Barry Trotter
and the Shameless
Parody

BARRY TROTTER
and the Shameless Parody

Michael Gerber

A MESSAGE FROM THE PUBLISHER OF THIS BOOK:
While the authentic series may or may not be Satanic, this book definitely is. It is poorly written, incredibly crass, and contains jokes about bodily functions that would embarrass a five-year-old. It has been produced as cheaply as possible, using highly toxic ink and substandard paper. Every corner has been cut, from eliminating every 500th word, to employing copy-editors fluent only in Spanish. This book exists soley to make a quick buck.

A MESSAGE FROM SATAN:
Oh, no, you're not pinning this one on me! This book totally *sucks*.

A MESSAGE FROM THE UNIVERSAL COUNCIL OF CHURCHES:
Any book so clearly loathed by Satan, the embodiment of all evil, logically must be the purest good. Otherwise, why would Satan hate it so? Therefore, I urge all right-thinking Christians, as well as people of goodwill from every other faith to read this parody.

A MESSAGE FROM YOUR LITTLE BROTHER:
This book is weird. I don't like it. Harry doesn't smoke. Smoking is for losers.

This edition published in 2003 by Gollancz

The right of Michael Gerber to be identified as the author
of this work has been asserted by him in accordance
with the Copyright, Designs and Patents Act 1988

First published in Great Britain in 2002 by Gollancz
An imprint of the Orion Publishing Group
Orion House, 5 Upper St Martin's Lane, London WC2H 9EA

Barry Trotter and the Shameless Parody
Summary: Fans of the world's most popular children's book are unfairly cheated after mistakenly purchasing a poorly-written, obnoxious spoof. They form a vigilante group and track down the author, executing him in a particularly unpleasant way.

A CIP catalogue record for this book
is available from the British Library

ISBN 0 575 07497 3

Typeset by Deltatype Ltd, Birkenhead, Merseyside

Printed in Great Britain by
Clays Ltd, St Ives plc

To Jon and Kate . . .
and J.K. Rowling, with impudent admiration.

'Adults are just obsolete children,
and to hell with them.'
— *Theodor Seuss Geisel (Dr. Seuss)*

Author's Note: Any instances of nonstandard
spelling, grammar, or punctuation are hereby
declared *intentional*, and should be considered jokkes.

CONTENTS

ONE   The Trouble with Muddles   1

TWO   The Butcher of Hogwash   20

THREE   Mr. Barry's Wild Ride   37

FOUR   A Visit With the Head Master   49

FIVE   The Right Snuff   64

SIX   The Pinewood Peckerwood   78

SEVEN   In the Belly of the Beast   96

EIGHT   For Some Reason, Dogs Figure Prominently
  in this Story   112

NINE   The Prisoner of Aztalan   129

TEN   Fantastic!   140

ELEVEN   Charlie and the Mildew-Infested Used
  Bookstore   149

TWELVE   The Great Escape   165

THIRTEEN   A Breaking Windfall   181

FOURTEEN   All A-Bored   199

FIFTEEN   Nightmares can be Extremely Instructive
   (Especially in Cheesy Books Like This One)   218

SIXTEEN   Relax, It's Later Than You Think   230

SEVENTEEN   Yes, Adulthood Stinks, But
   Consider The Alternative   246

EPILOGUE   266

Chapter One

THE TROUBLE
WITH MUDDLES

〰️

The Hogwash School for Wizards was the most famous school in the wizarding world, and Barry Trotter was its most famous student. His mere presence made sure that each year, twenty candidates applied for every open spot, no matter how rapacious Hogwash's tuition became. As a result, Barry and the school had come to an unspoken agreement: regardless of his grades, Barry could remain at Hogwash as long as he wished. He had just begun his eleventh year. This arrangement made studying unnecessary, and turned each evening from a time of frenzied scholarship to one of relaxed contemplation of the day's events. There was also ample time for mischief.

Sprawled sideways across an overstuffed chair in the Grittyfloor Common Room, in front of a cozy multicoloured fire, Barry silently pitied the other students. And the teachers, too – anyone, in fact, who didn't have it as immaculately cushy as he did. He turned up the headphones playing his favorite band, Valid Tumor Alarm, a group so deeply hostile that any song without the word 'kill' in the title was automatically classified as a ballad.

'We collect our Fear and turn it into a God,' Barry read. I wonder what the hell that means? His mind began to wander, as it usually did when confronted with a difficult thought.

Putting down his copy of *Existentialism for Beginners*, he pulled his wizard pipe from his pocket. He had bought it last week in Catty Corner, the magical shopping district down in London. Barry thought it gave him an air of mystery and maturity, the only things that perpetual student status did not confer. Girls seemed to agree. (Well, Muddle ones, at least.)

Wizard pipes were leagues better than the Muddle version; they weren't addictive, nor did they lead to galloping mouth rot. They also never had to be filled. Barry clenched the little wonder between his teeth.

'*Colibri!*'

The pipe lit itself, and a skein of smoke curled upward. The bowl was made of the finest magical meerschaum, which, as advertised, began to carve itself into an exact replica of its owner. 'Cool!' Barry said, taking it out for a second to look at the forming portrait. There was even a tiny pipe sticking out of the portrait's mouth – on which, Barry supposed, an even smaller portrait was forming . . . boy, a thought like that could break your brain.

Barry coughed. He had never actually lit the pipe before, preferring to use it simply as a prop; besides playing with the smoke, he couldn't figure out the appeal. His mouth tasted like he was chewing tree bark. The smoke *was* fun – wizard pipe smoke could be formed into any shape you wanted. Barry gave himself a sombrero, an arrow through the head, and a devil's horns in quick succession.

As he puffed, Barry could see this book's already slim chance at a Newlyburied medal quite literally going up in smoke. Well, he thought, if I'm screwed already, I might as well go have some fun.

'Bloody—' an ash had spilled onto his lap. He brushed frantically, but it was too late; a small hole had been burned in his father's old Cape of Invisibility. 'Damn!' Barry said. 'I'd better put this bugger out before it sets me on fire.' The pipe extinguished itself and Barry slipped it into his pocket, then pitched his book into the fire. It was magical, so it screamed.

Belching up a little institutional-grade rice pudding, Barry slipped on his Cape of Invisibility and walked towards the front door of Hogwash. He was the epitome of laziness, except when it came to getting into trouble, making a little money, or both at once; he delighted in seeing just how far he could push old Bumblemore and the rest. His first few terms had been pleasant, in that ooh-look-there's-that-famous-kid sort of way – lots of ogling and jockeying for his approval, the occasional theft of his knickers and speedy resale of same on eBuy. But then, in exchange for a few hundred pounds, some journo friend of his Muddle Aunt and Uncle wrote a couple of (mostly fictional) books about his life. Then things got interesting.

Near the front door, Almost Brainless Bill glided by, dragging his cerebellum and spinal cord behind him like a child's pull-toy. It left a trail of spectral slime. Barry took care not to bump into the spirit and arouse suspicion – although last time he did, he uttered a soft 'Moo!' and ever since Bill had believed that an invisible ghost cow walked the halls of the school. 'I shudder to think what heinous circumstances led to her spirit's imprisonment in these dank halls. Murder, perhaps? Or a doomed love affair?' Bill had said at dinner a few

days later, while Barry pulled a stomach muscle trying
not to laugh.

Outside of the school now, he moved through the
muddy, smelly crowd of youngsters with a quick step.
He could never get used to the rankness that assaulted
him every evening. Were *everybody's* fans this gross? It
was not merely an unpleasant ripeness borne of too
many people living too close together with no sanita-
tion facilities, but a pervasive, penetrating, unnerving
funk that seemed to suggest a widely-held organic
disorder. Tonight, the tell-tale stench of roast centaur
also hung in the air. Mixed with the aftertaste of pipe
tobacco, it was unspeakably horrid. He coughed, and
spat to get the smell out of his mouth. The gobbet
landed on a small, thin, bespectacled girl who sat
crosslegged on a patch of dirt re-reading a worn copy
of Barry Trotter and the Philosopher's Scone.[1] She

---

[1] This book was released as *Barry Trotter and the Magic Biscuit* in
America. As readers of the first book know, the Philosopher's Scone
contained the Elixir of Life, making anyone who ate it immortal.
(This is not to be confused with the Elixir of Lust, which makes
people immoral. Big difference.) Anyway, the Philosopher's Scone
seemed like a great career opportunity to the evil Lord Valumart,
who considered compound interest the only power greater than
himself – gaining immortality gave the investment strategy 'buy and
hold' a whole new meaning. Anyway, after Barry thwarted
Valumart, Bumblemore locked the pastry in his desk. He meant to

felt her hair, then looked skyward. Barry laughed. If she only knew, she'd never wash her hair again!

Barry reached the Forsaken Forest. At a clearing just inside it stood Hafwid, the school's giant game-keeper, surrounded by twenty or so women of all sizes and complexions. Two centaurs, Thelonious and Bird, stood talking to Hafwid, smoking tiny cigarettes. Seldom without berets and *never* without shades, centaurs are the hipsters of the magical world.

Barry slipped off his cloak, and all the Muddle females gasped as one. He never tired of that.

'Well, well, Slim's here to get some slickum on the hangdown,' Thelonious said.

'Hey T, Bird. Slip me some hoof. Who's out there on the spit?'

'That there's Diz. Never did care for him.' Thelonious looked over his sunglasses at Barry. 'JAMF, if you ask me.'

'Time for us cats to split,' said Bird, and he and Thelonious adjusted their berets and cantered into the woods. In the distance, a lone bongo drum could be heard.

throw it out, but eventually a mouse got to it and became immortal. The other mice logically proclaimed him the Messiah, and ever since, a dangerous cult had been growing inside the walls and wainscoting of Hogwash.

Barry turned to the giant gamekeeper. 'Thanks, Hafwid, ol' buddy,' he said, flipping a coin to the king-sized oaf, who fumbled it. 'You know the drill: go hang out with your pet bogarts[2] for an hour or two.'

Hafwid picked up the coin, and bit it. 'T'anks, Barry,' he said, and stumbled uncertainly into the forest, clutching a bottle wrapped in brown paper.

Another night, another gaggle of groupies. By now, it bored Barry stiff, but in some weird way, it was how he reminded himself he was a celebrity, somebody special. And (he rationalized) talk about giving back to your fans! 'Okay, girls: line up for your de-lousing spell, and then we can get started,' Barry said. 'Did everybody remember to wash?'

The next morning at breakfast, Barry was describing his exploits in graphic detail to a group of rapt sycophants. As was customary, they were showered with well-deserved disapproval from Hogwash's female contingent. Just as a particularly indignant fifth-year named Penelope Bluggs was preparing a Itching Madness spell, the morning owls arrived. Everyone quickly covered their glasses and bowls from

[2] A bogart is a shape-shifter that takes on the form of your worst fear – personified as your least favorite actor.

the flurry of feathers and mites and such that accompanied every delivery. Owls were a filthy way to deliver the mail.

Barry got a letter from the headmaster. He showed it to the group.

'Maybe it's good news. Maybe old Snipe's got cancer of the wand,' said Manuel Rodriguez, a third-year who will not reappear, but was shoehorned in so that not *everybody* in this story was white, middle-class, and British.

'Not likely – it's a yowler.' Barry opened it. 'See me immediately!' it boomed. 'And bring that good-for-nothing Lon with you!' There were scattered giggles, which Barry silenced with a mean look and trademark gesture.

Lon Measly, Barry's boon companion, was indeed good-for-nothing. Or very little, at least. He had suffered a tragic Quiddit accident during fifth year – a Basher had whiffed on a Brainer, causing it to lodge in Lon's noggin at great speed. All attempts to remove the ball had caused it to work its way in further; it finally came out the other side, so that Lon's head had a peephole pushed through it about the size of a one-pound coin. (When the wind hit it just right, it whistled.) Nurse Pommefritte had jerry-rigged him a new brain, using the barely-adequate faculties of a hastily-euthanized golden retriever. Lon was left with the capacities of a dim, good-natured seven year-old, and some definite canine tendencies.

'Come on,' Barry said, distracting Lon from the eternal quest to lick himself. 'Fuzzface wants to see us.' Lon smelled worse than usual. 'Have you been rolling in raccoon poop again?' Lon also chased cars. On the other hand, he was extremely loyal.

Penelope's Itching Madness spell thwacked on the wall behind them as they left the room. 'Pigs!' she yelled.

'Pffft.' Alpo Bumblemore shuffled the cards as he watched the Woodstock-like scene below. He picked a card. 'Ace of Clubs? No. Damn.' There had been a tent city of the most unattractive sort on the lawn of Hogwash for weeks now, ever since someone had published directions to the school in *The Stun*. 'Stunningly insipid!' was the paper's motto, one it lived up to – or, more accurately, down to – every day. Its primary claim to fame was that all the women in its pages were computer-enhanced so as to appear naked. This did wonders for circulation, except when Margaret Thatcher made news.

Anyway, Hogwash's lawn had been churned to ankle-deep muck almost immediately by the masses of

Chapter One

Stun-reading, Barry-loving Muddles encamped upon it. Bumblemore grimaced as someone brazenly relieved themselves in the lake. He mumbled a word, and a small lamprey-like sea monster attached itself to the offending part. 'That'll teach you,' Bumblemore said aloud.

Bumblemore heard a splash; Muddles had been pushing each other off Hogwash's high cliff at the rate of 5 an hour. The resident kraken was eating well. One of its tentacles held an encouraging placard saying 'JUMP!' Unfortunately, this didn't thin their numbers – more fans were arriving every day.

Hippies, the headmaster thought, seeing a pair of fans making 'the book with two covers' in the grass. Drug addicts. D&D players. He'd turn them all to cinders if he could, even the ones who were just bookish kids with a weakness for hero-worship and savvy merchandising. But there were a fair number of adults in the crowd, too. Perhaps fans of the books, perhaps Manson-like wolves moving among the sheep.

'Oh, well,' he said. 'God protects drunks, blondes and Muddles.' An ace fell from Bumblemore's voluminous sleeve. 'There you are, you rascal.'

Is this about the girls, or selling the map, or something else bad I did, but forgot? Barry wondered as he and

Lon climbed the crumbling stairs to Bumblemore's office. If it was the map, nobody could blame him; he *needed* that money. His godfather Serious Blech had sunk his entire inheritance into a harebrained scheme which failed, and Barry had long since burned through the money that J.G. Rollins gave him for telling his life story. A whole summer in the Muddle world – in its Dimsley-encrusted armpit, no less – required many cigarettes and much lager to endure.

But Bumblemore wouldn't buy that. He'd wanted Barry to shove off last year. 'Nobody ever in the history of Hogwash has been held back for five years in a row!' he had yelled. 'Trotter, you're a disgrace. I know you're doing it on purpose. All this publicity has turned you into a cosmically-lazy, slightly magical slacker. Do us all a favor and switch over to the Dork side – they'll never recover!'

The musty old wizard was right, and Barry would be the first to admit it. But who could blame Barry for staying a student? He was a king here, a god. Famous, surrounded by easy marks who were all too willing to loan cars, do laundry, or any other favor for the great Barry Trotter. Life can only go downhill from here, he thought.

At least from Barry's perspective, this latest scam had worked out brilliantly. Not only had he been well paid for the map, but now he had a rag-tag, fetid mob of his fans encamped on Hogwash's front lawn. No instructor dared fail him with a 5,000-strong pro-Trotter vandal army so close at hand.

However, even he was beginning to get a little annoyed. Their constant, moronic chants of love added sonic unpleasantness to the visual element so amply supplied by their unsafe, rickety lean-tos and unimaginably tatty appearance. They were obnoxious and smelly – then they had discovered Hafwid's still, and the mass brawling had begun.

Hafwid's liquor supply was nothing any sane person would mess with; if Hafwid didn't get you, the jet-fuel like spirits would. An apologetic jeroboam of magic 900-proof brandy patched things up, between him and Barry at least – Hafwid still despised the Muddles, and they seemed to know it somehow, singling him out for torment. Hafwid's Blast-Ended Brewts sent a few intruders to the hospital, and some others went blind from drinking raw alcohol, but Barry knew he had fans to burn.

Boy, these stairs were taking a long time. 'I wish this narration would hurry up,' he said. Lon whimpered in incoherent agreement.

As they approached the door to Bumblemore's

office, they were dive-bombed by a flock of pickpocketing bats lurking in the shadows. Whatever booty these thieving marsupials got, they took back to Grittyfloor's rival house, Silverfish, and woe betide any student that tried to get anything back. They didn't mess with Barry, but Lon was a favorite target, since he often carried old food in his pockets. Waving their arms frantically, they ran towards Bumblemore's door. It opened automatically.

'Trotter—'

Barry and Lon stopped, and the door swung shut. Barry panted, 'Professor, I just want you to know that I was interviewing all those girls for the school newspaper.'

Bumblemore turned. He looked very fed up. 'Trotter, you know very well we don't have a school paper, and if Muddle girls have the bad judgment to let you within 50 feet of them, they deserve what they get. This is altogether more serious. Come over to the window.'

The pair looked down at the chanting, moshing mass of mud-covered Muddledom. There were thousands of them, and not a Porta-Potty in sight. The smell was almost visible, like heat coming off a road.

'Look at these muttonheads. It's like a bloody Renaissance Faire down there,' Bumblemore grumbled. 'Do you know I had to deliver a baby this morning? Very messy business, Muddle birth. They named it Barry, of course. I was so appalled I nearly threw up on it.'

Barry leaned out of the window, which galvanized the crowd. A great ragged cheer rose up. Misspelled banners unfurled. 'Go away!' Barry yelled.

'He says we can stay!' said a Muddle. 'Hurrah! Hurrah for Barry Trotter!'

'Idiot!' Bumblemore spat at our hero. 'Now we'll never be rid of them.' He grabbed Barry's elbow. 'Get away from that window before you do more damage.'

Quick as a flash, Bumblemore licked his thumb, raised Barry's fringe and rubbed the scar on his forehead. The mark, in the shape of an Interrobang,[3] was the result of Barry's battle with Lord Valumart while an infant. It was also his proof of wizarding greatness, and Bumblemore was convinced it was a mistake.

'Get off!' Barry said, pushing the mothball-and-patchouli-scented magi-git away.

They turned to see Lon putting the small end of

---

[3] In the Muddle world, the Interrobang is a failed piece of punctuation, half question mark, half exclamation point. As in 'What the Hell was that?!' or 'I just ate WHAT?!' Being both chronically confused and easily excitable, Barry's mother felt an affinity with the Interrobang. Thus, Barry was marked with one.

Bumblemore's telescope into his mouth. Since the accident, Lon was a great gnawer.

'Lon! *No!*'

Lon, startled, knocked over a tin of magic ants which spilled all over the floor. They began to spell out dirty words on the floor.

The aged headmaster struggled to control his temper. 'Look, you two – I want you to listen, so you can get the blazes out of my office.' In the corner, Bumblemore's pet phoenix Sparky, flickered as it pecked at an asbestos cuttlebone.

Bumblemore brandished a copy of *The Stun*. 'Someone – I suspect the latest odious issue of the Malfeasance clan currently oozing all over Silverfish House' – Barry hoped his relief didn't show – 'has given this paper the directions to Hogwash. Ergo, those pinheads down there.' He threw *The Stun* in the wastepaper basket with great force. 'I am getting entirely too old for this pile of fewmets.'

With the threat of punishment receding, Barry's mind had wandered. His eyes played over the titles in Bumblemore's bookshelves . . . *She Wore a Golden Whip; Miss Harriet's Torture Closet;* and Barry's favorite, *Prisoner at a Women's College, or the Private Diary of Phineas Bantam-Pullet, Flagellant*. The first-year Barry had been shocked; eleven years later, he was just amused – Bumblemore had an odd idea of fun, but who doesn't? The slap of paper against wastebasket shook Barry from his reverie, and he heard Bumblemore say, 'Our deceptive spells are useless; it takes basic intelligence to be deceived, and those knuckleheads simply ain't got.'

'How could someone do something like that? And for what? A bit of money!' Barry snorted derisively, laying it on thick. 'There's more to life than money, I always say, don't I, Lon?'

'Yep,' Lon sputtered, a spindle of drool sliding from his chin.

'God, what a dolt you are, Measly.' Bumblemore paused a moment, eyes closed, squeezing the bridge of his nose, then said, 'Pardon me. This infernal chanting has given me a splitting headache. As bad as things are right now, they may get much, much worse – if today's *Daily Soothsayer* is right.' He grabbed the paper off his desk and handed it to Barry.

'POOP,' spelled the ants.

'What? "Sex-for-Grades Scandal Rocks Academic World"?' Barry asked, reading a headline.

'No, below that,' Bumblemore said.

'"New Penalties for Sodomy Called 'Unimaginably Draconian'"?'

'Let me see that!' Bumblemore exclaimed, grabbing

the paper back. He scanned in vain – Barry had made that one up. 'You think you're so funny,' Bumblemore groused. He jabbed at an article. '*That* one.'

'"Brit Wiz Whiz Flick Picked to Click,"' Barry read. 'All of Tinseltown is buzzing about the movie, "Barry Trotter and the Inevitable Attempt to Cash In," slated for release in just one month. Fans of the children's fantasy series are expected to mob theaters worldwide.

'Wagner Brothers is betting on the big-budget biopic, hoping that an all-out promotional and merchandising blitz will make the movie a massive international hit, even bigger than the publishing phenomenon that spawned it.'

'I don't understand,' Barry said. 'This seems like it can only help Hogwash. You know what they say, "No publicity is bad publicity."'

Bumblemore smacked his forehead at Trotter's stupidity; as he did so, a single blue moth skittered upwards from his robes. 'Trotter, you are a fool. How many kids actually read books these days? One in ten? A hundred? And yet, look outside—' as he pulled aside the curtain, a handful of something hit the window. (It wasn't mud.)

'We want Barry!' the crowd yelled.

Bumblemore made a rude gesture to the crowd, which booed him lustily. 'Do you have *any* idea how many people will show up here after the movie? Adding in overseas, home video, and DVD rentals, maybe a hundred million people will see it. That means we'll have 500,000 people of all ages fighting, singing, bleeding and God-knows what else-ing on our lawn by Boxing Day.'

'UH-OH,' the ants spelled, until Lon, giggling, decimated the last 'H' with his foot.

The enormity of it broke in Barry's mind, and a trickle of sweat rolled down his scalp. 'Why not just move Hogwash? Magically, I mean?'

'Insurance,' Bumblemore said. 'Our lawyers at Warlocke and Wyvern tell me that it would break us to move. We might as well close the school altogether, and go back to correspondence courses. Anyway, since you're the cause of all of this, I want you to fix it. Stop that movie, Barry Trotter, or Hogwash is history.'

'But if a Malfeasance was the one who—' said Barry shamelessly.

'His parents are Trustees,' Bumblemore said. 'Your parents are mulch.'

'Okay, okay.' This could be my next book, Barry thought, mental cash registers ringing. I'll call J.G., and – no. It was that kind of thinking that had gotten them into this mess. 'Can Lon help? And Ermine?'

'As our only Special Ed student, I doubt very much

Lon will be missed. The experience may be good for him. Miss Cringer is teaching at a remedial wizards school outside Hogsbleede; whether she can help or not is up to her.'

A knock came on the door, and Hafwid stumbled in. As usual, he was wearing a battered baseball cap advertising a brand of dragon feed. 'P'rfes'r Bummlemore, sum of thos' Muddles done broke into my cab'n agin! Thair pawin' through mah smalls!' Hafwid's 'smalls' were as big as a pup tent. 'Can I kill 'um?'

'Son of a witch,' Bumblemore muttered. 'No, Hafwid, I'll handle it.' He moved to the door, then turned back and said, in an almost fatherly way, 'Barry, the school is depending on you. If you ever get into a tight spot and think you might not be able to stop the movie, I want you to remember one thing . . .' He put his hand on Barry's shoulder. '. . . if Hogwash closes, you'll have to go get a job.' Then he and Hafwid left.

Lon scooped a handful of ants into his mouth, leaving 'SHI' on the carpet. 'Yuck,' he said, sticking out his tongue.

'My thoughts exactly,' said Barry.

Chapter Two

THE BUTCHER
OF HOGWASH

〰️

After corralling the profane ants, Barry and Lon left Bumblemore's study. They made quite sure the door was locked – the last time that Sparky got loose, most of Pufnstuff House was reduced to charred rubble. For something that was mostly mouldy rock, these old castles sure could burn.

Lucky for the boys, most of the larcenous bats had fallen into a light slumber, and the few that were still awake were preoccupied with smoking cigarettes, looking tough, and trying to rob each other. Barry and Lon tiptoed past, leaving them to their fluttery squabbling.

As readers of *Barry Trotter and the Chamberpot of Secrets* already know, Bumblemore often answered Nature's call by means of an amazingly lifelike porcelain reproduction of Barry's head. Bumblemore had placed it in the hall for a house-elf to empty; as if radar-guided, Lon's shin upended it, knocking it down the stairs with a splash and smash. The roused bats flew at them. 'Run!' Barry yelled.

Barry spied a door slightly ajar down the hall. 'Quick, in here!' he cried, and Lon piled in behind him. They both regretted it immediately.

'Oh, GOD!' Barry said. 'Of all the rooms to pick.' It was the dreaded Upper South Bathroom, home to one of Hogwash's least-loved spirits, Flatulent Fanny.

'Who's out there?' a quavering, high-pitched voice cried from one of the stalls. The air was rank with the fruits of Fanny's ghostly intestine.

'Ohhh,' Fanny moaned, as another gastric salvo sputtered to life. 'Go away, I feel sick.'

'P.U.' said Lon, pinching his nose. 'Blap,' Fanny 'replied.'

'Fanny, whatever you're eating, *stop*!' Barry yelled, breathing through his mouth. The bats outside beat their tiny bodies against the door in a Morse code of stupidity.

'Don't yell at me. Everybody hates me [ploot!] but it's not my fault,' Fanny said weakly. 'I'm lactose-intolerant [brrrip].' Fanny was a first-year who had died in 1952, after some Silverfish third-years hid a massive amount of cheese in her dinner one evening. As she crampily met her Maker, she swore vengeance, and each of the bullies were driven mad by a mysterious, visible stench which trailed them wherever they went. No breeze could move it, no soap could remove the sulphurous signature of Fanny's unhappy gut – death was the only relief. After her tormentors had done away with themselves, Fanny took up residence in the bathroom where she had expired. Ironically, locking first-years in with Fanny had become a favorite trick of Hogwash's bullies.

Slowly, the beating of the bats stopped. Barry opened the door a crack, letting in a trickle of sweet, fresh air. The coast was clear.

'Okay, Lon, let's go,' he said. 'Seeya, Fanny.'

'Nobody likes me,' Fanny said. The rest of her sentence was obscured by an abdominal outburst.

As Lon and Barry turned a corner, they were suddenly confronted by one of Hogwash's most color-ful denizens, the semi-feral Mrs. McGoogle. Once leader of Grittyfloor and a productive member of the Hogwash faculty, the now spectacularly-unkempt McGoogle had been unhinged by the constant stream of dramatic events that Trotter and his cronies had unleashed upon the school. After years of mayhem – from Lord Valumart's constant, clumsy attempts to do away with Barry, to Ferd and Jorge Measly's endless barrage of asinine pranks and now, finally, the appearance of the unwashed masses at the school's very gates – her hyper-orderly mind snapped. Overnight, the formidable Mrs. McGoogle turned into a world-class nutter, skulking around the school dressed in a discarded flour sack, subsisting somehow on the leavings in student trashcans. It was a medical miracle she had lasted this long; people whispered that Bumblemore kept her in a secret sex dungeon, where the wizened, barmy pervert aired a set of privates too wrinkly to contemplate. Once quite a powerful wizard, McGoogle now transformed into a cat only when she went into 'heat,' which, at her age, was blessedly seldom.

'Boo,' Barry wheezed, out of breath. The addlepated woman hissed, spraying Barry with sour-smelling spit, and spun on her heel. She skittered away, her long toenails clicking double-time down the corridor. The bats reversed direction and followed her, a stupid choice since she had nothing but her wits and precious few of those. Barry and Lon heard her footfalls recede, then what sounded like a crash as La McGoogle careened into some metal something some distance away.

'Barry, how long will we be gone?' Lon asked.

'Stopping the movie? I don't know.'

'Because I want to get my hat from my room.'

'Good thinking,' Barry said. Lon's hat, a double-coned Laplander knit cap with reindeer on it, was essential for their trip into the Muddle world; its ample flaps covered the hole through his head, and muffled its cheerful bottle-like note. 'Before we do that, though,' Barry said, 'I'd like to stop by Zed's.'

Zed Grimfood was Hogwash's armorer, an ex-Error fired by the Ministry after killing too many Muddles in his war against the Earth Eaters.[4] Zed had always held it against Barry that he'd never made it into the books; he fancied himself the very model of a tough action star.

Barry didn't blame J.G. Rollins for not putting him in – Zed was a paragon of bad judgment, a parent's nightmare, pure sales poison. Crude, quick to fight, incredibly hostile, the palest caricature of Zed would instantly remove the series from school libraries all over the world. Heck, Zed was too intense for *Barry*, the guy who regularly doled out noogies to the Dork Lord. As written, the Trotter series was strictly PG-rated, and old Zed was an ostentatious 18 (excessive

---

[4] They were called this because Lord Valumart made them eat copious amounts of dirt as proof of their loyalty to him.

violence, adult situations). And if he ever veered into X, Barry didn't want to know.

'Why do we need to see Zed?' Lon asked. He was afraid of Zed to the point of pants-wetting – which, it must be admitted, came a lot easier to Lon than most.

'Because if we tell him what we're doing, perhaps he'll give us something helpful,' Barry said. 'Or something we can sell.'

'For gum?' Lon loved chewing gum.

'Yes, possibly.'

'Goody,' said Lon, then paused. 'But what are we *doing*, Barry?'

'Didn't you listen to Bumblemore? We're going to stop the movie?'

'How?' Lon asked.

Barry didn't know, so he made something up. 'We're going to kidnap J.G. Rollins,' Barry said.

'Oh,' Lon said.

Barry and Lon's ears had not deceived them: Mrs. McGoogle had crashed into a haunted suit of armour. Its ghost was picking up the pieces, grumbling all the while. 'Blamed fleshies, think they can just run into people . . . no respect for the dead . . .'

Behind the ghost stood a door which had a brass plate reading, *Zed Grimfood, Armourer*. 'Excuse us,' Barry said, pushing the flimsy pieces of display armour to the side with his foot. 'Watch it,' the ghost said petulantly. 'That's me 'ome you're kickin'.'

'Mr. Grimfood,' Barry said, knocking normally. 'It's Barry Trotter and Lonald Measly.' The whine and grind of heavy machinery could be heard. Then, after there was no answer, he pounded on the door, shouting, 'Mr. Grimfood!'

Barry and Lon heard the machinery abruptly cut off, then heard Zed's girlishly high voice cry out, 'Back, ye devils!'

The door opened, and there stood Zed, all six foot nine inches of him. He was a big, hairy man, with a long, red, forked beard. His facial hair was so impressive that he made the frizzy Bumblemore look like a piker. In addition to his forked beard, Grimfood had forked sideburns. His head hair was separated into many tufts, each tied with a small ribbon, which stuck out like a child's drawing of the sun. The whole effect was kind of pirate-y, with heavy overtones of a bizarro sexuality Barry shuddered to contemplate. His bear-like bulk was clothed in a smudged denim apron, and he beat back a swarm of translucent pixies with a freckled paw. They dodged it easily, snickering and taunting.

'Why, if it isn't Trotter. And Lon. Come in,' Zed offered a greasy hand, which promptly crushed Barry's in a prehistoric show of dominance. He was holding a pink featherduster, which was apparently the source of all that racket. 'Hello, Sir Cyril,' Zed said to the ghost. 'I see Cyclone McGoogle's been here.'

'Some people shouldn't 'ave bodies,' Sir Cyril said, his arms full of armor. 'Some people aren't *responsible* enough.' 'Quite,' said Zed, and closed the door. 'Pillow-biter,' Zed mumbled to himself.

'Don't mind the pixies,' he said to the boys. 'That curse is a royal pain, it is.' He tossed them two pairs of plastic safety goggles. 'Put these on,' Zed said. 'They like to lay their eggs in the fluid of your eyes.'

'Ahhh!' Barry and Lon squinted immediately, and scrambled to put on the glasses. Professor Snipe, Hogwash's evil-tempered Professor of Notions, had given Zed a chronic case of the pixies after a dust-up several years ago. Nobody would lift the curse for fear of crossing Snipe, and it really curtailed Zed's success with the ladies.

The dumb little pixies smacked into their safety goggles incessantly. You got so as you didn't even see it.

'I see you're still wearing your glasses, Barry,' Zed said. 'I wish you'd let me do something about that.' Zed had offered, many times, to make Barry a new pair of magical all-zinc eyeballs. Barry, sensibly, had declined.

Chapter Two

Grimfood stood in his fluorescently-lit, concrete-floored workroom, surprisingly up-to-date for Hogwash, where the plumbing and wiring was quintessentially English. (Bumblemore was constantly calling the house elves in to fix this or that thing, but they were unionized and often on strike, so everybody had learned to accept unflushing toilets and small electrical fires – and incredibly, unflushing spark-throwing toilets – as part of life.[5]) Zed wiped his hands on his apron, which was so smudged with grease (and blood? it sure looked like it) that they came back dirtier than before.

There, stretched out on Zed's worktable, utterly defenseless, was a blow-up sex doll. It wasn't very high-quality; Barry bet it wouldn't last thirty seconds under Zed's writhing bulk. Barry lifted a deflated arm. 'What are you doing with your friend here, Zed?' Barry asked. 'Dusting?'

---

[5] It must be admitted that Hogwash was crumbling in no small part thanks to Bumblemore's terrifying ineptitude as a fundraiser. It was difficult under any circumstances, since most of the Trustees were pals of Valumart (because, let's face it – you can't amass a sizeable fortune without being at least a little Dork). But Bumblemore's tendency to give the more bothersome of them the ol' one-finger salute kept the Trustees in a constant state of near revolt. They were, in fact, secretly funding the revolutionary mice.

'Put that down!' Zed said testily. 'That's personal, that is!' He grabbed it and stuffed it into a box.

'You really don't pay attention in class, do you, Trotter? This isn't a featherduster, it's an Enchantomatic.' He took his wand from behind his ear and fit it into the end of the duster. 'This focuses the magic juice. Then, you get whatever object you want to enchant' – he fished a Boarsbollocks' Brew bottlecap from his pocket and placed it on the table – 'put the duster directly over it, and . . .' There was a flash, and a smell of ozone. 'It's enchanted.'

The bottlecap gave a squeak, and began to hop about, bending itself in half like a mouth with every jump. Zed squashed it with a meaty fist. It gave a little shriek, then moved no more. Lon felt sad. Barry felt sorry for the latex lady fated to play Pinocchio to Zed's booty-starved Geppetto. In the best public school tradition, there was something about Hogwash that encouraged kinkiness. All those rules, all those teenage hormones . . . the students usually came out okay, but the staff were all strange, sexually (and otherwise), almost without exception.

'What can I do for you, boys?'

Lon jumped right in. 'We're going to kidnap somebody!' This explained nothing for Zed, who looked at Barry, puzzled.

'We've got to go out into the Muddle world – maybe even to America – to prevent some people from making a movie about me,' Barry said. Feeling sure that he wouldn't be in this project, either, all the helpfulness drained from Zed's manner.

'Well, I can't see how the lowly Hogwash Armourer can help you with that,' Zed said. 'Now, if you'll excuse me, I have this lollipop to disarm.' He picked up what appeared to be a standard lollipop. It was covered with foreign writing, and through a gap in the wrapper, Barry could see that the candy was fiery orange.

Lon's eyes brightened. 'Oooh! Can I have it?'

'No, Lon,' Zed replied, smiling at him. 'It could be lethal. Your rascally brothers left it in their secret candy stash by the Iron Maria on the second floor, and a third-year found it. Almost ate it, too. No telling what could've happened then,' Zed said. Barry agreed – eating any candy that had passed through the hands of Ferd and Jorge Measly was a bad idea. He remembered the sweets they passed out to the first-years a few years back. Camouflaged as a delicious chocolate truffle, it caused monarch butterflies to hatch in your guts and stream out of your bottom. It was marvellous!

Zed stepped towards the door. 'I'll be up all night as it is, so if you'll excuse me . . .'

'Wait! Mr. Grimfood, listen,' said Barry, concocting a suitable lie, 'the reason we've got to stop this movie is that we've seen the screenplay and, well, it gets it all wrong. Certain people are missing, important people' – Zed brightened – 'and we are going there to make sure they're in it, and get the recognition they deserve.'

'Hm, well, in that case . . .' Zed tried to conceal his upsurge of interest by using the muscles of his right ear to pop the wand nestled behind it into the air, then catching it with his hand. This nervous habit was impressive enough the first time you saw it, but after a whole semester of Magickal Shop, it was simply irritating. 'What can I do for you?'

What a sucker, Barry thought, and reeled him in. 'We need some things for our mission. Things to help us if the going gets rough.'

'How about this saw?' Zed said, hoisting an eight-foot silver halberd into the air. 'You flip a switch here on the handle and—' The blade at the pole's end began to whirl with an awful buzz.

'Best saw in the world. Cuts through anything!' Zed shouted. 'This will persuade those Hollywood types!'

Lon, smiling broadly, hands clapped over his ears, hopped up and down. Loud noises excited him. Barry did not share his enthusiasm. 'No thanks,' he shouted. 'We need something smaller! More concealable!'

'Suit yourself!' Zed said. Distracted by the racket, he put the saw down before switching it off. It was as good as advertised, cutting through the floor effort- lessly with a spray of concrete chips. There was a scream from the classroom below. Zed yanked it backwards, and switched it off. 'Sorry,' he yelled.

'Turn it on again!' Lon yelled. He was ignored.

'Zed, do you have anything concealable?'

'I've got a thigh holster for your wand. Helps if you're ever frisked. Want it?'

'Sure,' said Barry. Zed tossed it to him. It was leather, and had a nude woman clumsily tooled into it. 'What about something that looks Muddle but isn't?' Zed reached a furry red arm into his apron pocket. He pulled out a pack of gum. 'How about this?'

'All *right!*' Lon hollered, excited. 'Now we don't have to sell—'

'Shut up, Lon,' fearing that Zed would catch on to his fencing scheme. 'Toss it over. Wait – it isn't going to explode or anything?'

'No, more's the pity.' Zed tossed it to Barry. It looked like gum, smelled like spearmint. 'It will clear out a room, however. It's tear gas gum; chew a piece, then breathe on somebody. They'll make way in a hurry.'

Barry was instantly charmed. He could get into real trouble with this. 'Great!' he said. 'Got anything else?'

Zed opened a many-drawered standing chest and started rooting around. 'It's the beginning of the term, so I don't have much . . . Serious Putty© – you don't want that. Magic slugs?'

'You mean like for slot machines?' Barry asked hopefully, thinking of a detour to Vegas.

'No, I mean like for gardens.'

'What do they do?' Barry asked, crestfallen.

'They write your name in slime. Very slowly. It's quite amusing if you have an afternoon to kill. Entirely non-lethal, though. What about this? Loyal jelly.' He turned, and tossed what looked like a toothpaste tube to Barry. Barry opened it and squeezed a little onto his fingertip. He immediately felt the sensation of being tongue-kissed on the finger.

'It's useful stuff. Made by a species of superaffectionate bee. There's nothing that jelly won't do for you.'

'But what *can* it do for you?' Barry asked.

'Stop leaks, protect your skin from heat or cold . . . say you have to fish a piece of toast out of the toaster. Squirt a little loyal jelly on your hand, and they'll gladly burn to death to protect the fingers of the one they love.'

Not really convinced of the product's usefulness, Barry tucked it into his pocket anyway. 'Thanks, Zed.'

As the adults talked, Lon was down on all fours, his nose at a mousehole, sniffing. Suddenly, a needle flew out of the hole, trailing thread. It hooked on Lon's collar, and there was a tiny cheer from inside the hole. Lon was so startled by this that he sprang to his feet and backed away. An old-fashioned flat roller skate, scrounged from somewhere, emerged from the hole, carrying seven mice. Lon turned and began to run.

'What else do you have?' Barry asked. 'I mean, if you can spare it. We'll take good care of anything you give us.'

'Aaaah!' Lon yelled, running past, trailing the zigzagging skate full of cheering mice.

'Not if you're using it right, you won't,' Zed laughed.

Still running around the room, Lon realized that the skate was attached to his collar, and began slapping at it. He dislodged the needle, and the mice were sent, their cheers now turned to screams, veering off into the wall. A few were injured, but none seriously. They weaved dizzily back to their hole, dragging the skate behind them.

Zed continued to root around in the nicked and spattered cabinet. 'Here, I've never even opened this. But it's good for incapacitating a Muddle or two.' He tossed a round brown and silver tin to Barry, who read, 'Phelgmberry Farms' Snot Chocolate.' He flipped it over. 'Inside this tin is the world's finest Snot Chocolate. This savory drink, a secret Phelgmberry family recipe, combines the richest, most finely-milled cocoa available, with an impossibly-powerful industrial-strength expectorant. Just one sip and you'll be saying, 'Mmmm . . . my sinuses are packed solid.' Your nose will run – gallop! – and you'll be hawking up fistfuls of creamy sputum for hours. Anytime's massive bogie time with Snotberry Farms!'

'I realize this is incredibly gross, Zed, but how could it help?'

Zed didn't look up. 'It will distract your assailant.'

Lon reached over. 'Mmm, smells like chocolate. Let me see.'

'No, Lon,' Barry said, whacking Lon lightly on the nose. 'Zed, what if I don't want to distract the Muddles. What if I need to splatter one all over the place?'

Zed turned, his eyes lit with glee – the thought of violence against Muddles warmed Zed's heart. 'I've got just the thing,' He pulled open a top drawer, and pulled out a vicious-looking, metallic pistol. Yes! Barry thought. *Here's* something I can pawn. '.357 Magnum.

Police issue, nickel finish. Snub-nosed for easy conceal-ment. You could stop a manticore with this baby,' purred Zed. He cocked it with a snap. 'Careful, it's loaded.' He tossed it to Barry before Barry could fathom what a bad idea that was.

Scared, Barry fumbled it, and they all dove for cover as it discharged. The bullet ricocheted, and – in a million to one shot – bounced cleanly through the newly-cut hole in the floor. A groan was heard, then Professor Snipe's voice, 'Cyril Broadbottom, I remind you that no one can be shot in my classroom without permission. Five points from Grittyfloor!'

Zed leaned over the hole and yelled, 'Sorry again!' He grimaced. 'Ew. Looks like that can splatter wizards, too. You guys had better go, before Snipe curses you, too.'

'Thanks, Zed,' Barry said, gathering up his loot. 'Wish us luck.'

'What happened?' said Lon, still in his defensive cower.

'Nothing, Lon. Good luck with your kidnapping,' Zed said. 'And Barry . . .'

'Yes?'

'If you can't stop it, and they make the movie anyway . . . well, could you make sure George Clooney plays me?'

Chapter Three

MR. BARRY'S
WILD RIDE

꧁ↀↀↀↄ꧂

Barry and Lon hurried out of Zed's office, just as real bedlam began to erupt. 'Now, see here, Grimfood, you can't go shooting one of my students!' they heard the exasperated Snipe shout before the door closed.

They took off their goggles and placed them by the door. 'This place is an asylum,' Barry said to Lon. Lon was unsure of the word 'asylum,' so he just smiled and nodded. It was amazing how far playing dumb could get you. He showed Barry the lollipop – he had swiped it off Zed's workbench in the commotion.

'Well, you are a Measly brother, aren't you? Good work. But I wouldn't eat that if I were you.'

'I CAN!' Lon said belligerently.

'Okay, but ask Ferd or Jorge first, okay?' Barry asked. 'Do you have to get anything from your room before we go?'

'Just my hat,' Lon said.

'Right, right,' Barry said. In addition to the essential flaps, Lon's hat had strings coming down that could be tied under his chin to keep the quasi-canine manchild's fuzz-covered jowls warm. But as it was only September, it was sure to look strange. Barry had quit caring ages ago.

'Okay, put that on, and get whatever else you want to bring, and I'll meet you at the portrait in five minutes,' said Barry. Lon went, his meandering sort of gait unsullied by any sense of purpose.

Barry headed towards his room. A first-year, Basil Basingstoke, passed him in the hall, carrying a round container. This gave Barry an idea.

'Hey, you – what's your name?'

'B-Basil,' Basil stammered, shocked that the great Barry Trotter was speaking directly to *him*.

'Yeh, Basil, give me that tin, would you?' Barry said.

'Oh, sure, Barry! Be glad to!' Basil immediately dumped its contents on the floor – he collected buttons – and handed it over. The buttons, enchanted, rolled away laughing, secreting themselves in every nook and cranny of the hallway. Basil would be rounding them up for hours.

'Thanks, kid,' Barry said, and continued walking to his room, knowing that Basil would gush to his friends about this chance encounter.

When Barry opened his door, he was greeted by the usual disaster area: an unmade bed smelling of sweat; carelessly taped-up posters for *Reservoir Dogs*, Bob Marley, and of course, a life-size one of Art Valumord, the lead singer of Valid Tumor Alarm; a broken lava lamp; a writing desk piled high with old assignments, angry letters, traffic tickets, bills and other trash; and his prize possession, a stolen street sign ('Road crumbles away into Pit of Hell, 5 km'). There were a few books, on shelves and in careless piles: some Camus and Hesse, never read; Salinger, Kerouac, Vonnegut, skimmed; Brautigan, from when he suspected he was deep enough to write poetry (he wasn't); lots of comics, and a subscription to *Viz* that his godfather Serious had gotten him ten years ago, which kept coming for some reason.

And of course there was his faithful owl, Earwig, who sat grumbling in her cage. Earwig had been confined to Barry's room since she went for Dorco Malfeasence's soft bits five years ago, and as usual, her cage was filthy. Barry's rule was: 'Don't clean it until your eyes water.'

Holding the fruitcake tin in one hand, he went over to Earwig's cage. Opening the door, he folded the corners of the feces-loaded newspaper over the top, making a bundle. He then deftly slid the bundle into the tin; the pile of droppings was a little higher than the tin, but he scrunched the lid down supertight. It was so full, he had to tape it shut.

Barry laughed to himself. It's the little pleasures in life that make the difference.

Taking some brown paper, he carefully wrapped the tin, then began to address the parcel. He stopped; this mustn't be traceable, thinking of the Muddle court order that had been passed a few years ago. Waving his wand, he mumbled the ancient summoning spell.

'Cmere!'

His magic pen unearthed itself from his desk and flew over to him. It stood poised over the package until Barry spoke: 'Mr. Vermon Dimsley, 4 Trivet Row, Piddlesex, England.' And, for the finishing touch, the return address was that of Uncle Vermon's boss. Barry smiled at the psychological damage he was about to inflict. Then, for some reason, he felt the tiniest twinge of conscience, which he squashed like a defenseless pixie.

Though his fans had been threatening them with death for years, Barry had been tormenting the Dimsleys as well, and rightly so. First, he had driven the obese, sadistic son insane by placing an endless loop of dogs barking 'Jingle Bells' in his head. Then, he had given the Missus a powerful sapphic crush on the Queen, which had the double benefit of not only ruining the Dimsleys' marriage (Vermon was driven into the arms of other even more shrewish and less attractive women), but also putting Mrs. Dimsley under 24 hour surveillance by MI5. To Barry's surprise, Vermon had proven to be the toughest of all three, like a cowpat baked rock-hard by a white-hot sun of obtuse stolidity.

'Here, Earwig. Muddle post, please,' Barry said, giving the owl the unpleasant task of ferrying her own droppings. But she was so glad to be free that she grabbed the twine with her talons without complaint, and swooped out of the window. She circled back to give Barry a dirty look, however, and he could've sworn that she stuck her tongue out at him. It was an inconvenient reality that his celebrity meant nothing to animals; they put up with less. Barry threw on his old Army jacket, which was ratty, and covered with ink blots from that brief period when he used fountain pens because they made him feel smart. He checked the pockets for various necessities (pipe, lighter, bottle opener, gun) and walked out.

Lon was waiting for him in front of the portrait in the Grittyfloor Common Room, cap on, ready to go. He was holding a thick book. Lon can't read an adult book like that, Barry thought. 'Hey, Lon, what's that for?'

'It's my journal,' Lon said. 'In case we have adventures.' Usually, Barry was much too protective of his brand identity to allow such a thing, but since it was Lon, who was still stuck on the cursive Q and therefore no threat to become an author, Barry decided not to be a sourpuss.

'After you,' Barry said. 'I see London, I see France,' Lon sang, and stepped into the painting, which obligingly lifted her hoop skirts and let him through. Barry followed, and the pair found themselves outside Hogwash. Barry threw the Cape of Invisibility over them both, so that the masses of Muddles milling about wouldn't see them. Unfortunately, Lon was considerably taller than Barry, so both pairs of legs showed from the knee.

'Follow me,' said Barry, heading to the Forsaken Forest.

'Barry, I don't think you should see your girlfriends right now!' Lon said with the peculiar moral intensity of the pre-pubescent. 'Shut up, stupid! We're going to get Ermine.' Lon was momentarily chastened, but soon lost himself in the myriad pungencies of the breeze.

Barry made sure he and Lon stayed far away from the infamous Buggering Birch. Whenever anyone would stray too close, this loathsome plant would reach out and – no, it's just too disgusting to describe.

'How are we going to get to Hogsbleede?' Lon asked.

'By hedgerow, of course,' Barry replied. Muddle England was covered with rows of large hedges, certainly large enough to cover an 'underground railroad,' especially if a little space-warping magic were applied. The wizarding community of England used this as their primary way to get around; Barry had forced J.G. Rollins to leave that part out of her books, as Muddle discovery of it would be a real headache – tolls, taxes, emissions tests and God knows what else. Still, it might not have mattered even if she had, since one of the things her mostly fanciful series got the rightest was this: *Muddles never pay any attention to anything but themselves*. And the ones that do look around, are dismissed as lunatics. 'A network of highways disguised as hedgerows, and used by magical people? Preposterous!' And it was, but that didn't make it any less true.

The hedge was a special variety; in addition to containing a form of mass transit, it produced leaves in the shape of letters. These letters, read in the correct order, formed words, and it was said that each hedge told its own unique story. Each fall, a masterpiece fell.

But each spring, new chapters sprouted. These stories didn't grow in the telling; they were told in the growing.

'This way in,' Barry read in leaves, as they arrived at the entrance to the hedgerow. Barry pulled off the Cape, and Lon lifted some outer branches to reveal a good-sized opening. (Some Muddles saw them appear out of thin air, but chalked it up to the undercooked, day-old centaur roiling in their bellies.) 'Thanks, Lon,' Barry said, and ducked inside. Lon followed.

They suddenly found themselves in a room, much bigger than a hedgerow, about as big as Grand Central Station, if you've ever been there. Barry always enjoyed the illusion when he made the shift. Most magic was pretty utilitarian, shabby even, but this was different, impressive. The effect of the sparkling lights peeping through the roof, a mass of branches and greenery, made one feel as if they were snuggled under a Christmas tree, getting sticky sap in their hair, ready to dodge falling ornaments.

At each corner of the square room, there was a line of toboggan-like vehicles, red two-seaters – one in the front, one in the back – with a vertical lever at the front for steering and for inclination control. A queue of magical, semi-magical, and wannabe creatures stood waiting for their turn in the toboggan rank. Somebody would get in to the toboggan, slide out of a tunnel-like opening in the chamber wall, and the next group would get in and do the same. It always reminded Barry of an amusement park ride.

The pair walked to the line under a large branch reading, 'Southeast Portal,' shuffling in behind a zoot-suited centaur, who twirled his long watch chain and tapped his hooves impatiently. The line moved slowly, but steadily, and soon Lon and Barry were climbing into their toboggan.

'Watch your step getting in,' the conductor said. The man's nose looked like it had been partially eaten away by some disease, and the rest of his face, while present, was similarly unwholesome. Barry didn't like the looks of him – or the toboggan, either: it was old, rusty, spotted with crude, flimsy patches and streaked with scorchmarks. There was a big hole in the floor board, and there looked to be a used condom in the backseat.

The interrobang on Barry's forehead throbbed a saucy samba of pain. He hesitated; should he ask for another toboggan?

'Step in, step in, got a whole line of people behind,' the conductor said, flashing a gapped grin that Barry thought was . . . evil? An image of this man flashed through his brain – scraggly, unshaven, wearing only a knee-length nightshirt and nightcap, the man danced in

the moonlight around a massive bonfire of books –
Barry's books. The shirt read, 'I Hate Barry Trotter!' in
large, black, iron-on letters. Cavorting demonically in
Barry's mind, he ripped off the shirt, howling like an
animal, revealing the grisly tattoo on his chest – a
picture of him, Barry, with a traffic-sign like circle and
diagonal line through it.

'I don't think we should take this—' Overcome by
pain, Barry swooned.

'Yer friend seems to've fainted,' the conductor said.
'I'll help you load 'im in.' Lon and the creepy transit
officer dumped the limp Barry into the backseat. Lon
assumed the controls, and the toboggan zoomed into
the tunnel, leaving the ghastly laughter of the conductor behind them. The branch over their head read,
'You'll be sorry' – but only Lon was awake to read it.

Barry came to, and was immediately confronted with
his worst nightmare: Lon at the wheel of a major
conveyance. Lon's brain injury had robbed him of any
perception of speed. Or momentum. Or balance. Also,
he was a little bit blind, even though he never admitted
it.

'Lon! Look out!' Barry yelled, as they narrowly
missed a bum sleeping it off against the wall of the

tunnel. Copies of the *Daily Soothsayer* went flying. 'Lon, let me —'

'Huh? *No*, Barry!' Lon bellowed; he was touchy about things like this. 'I can drive! I can *do* it!'

'Listen, nano-brain . . .' Barry reached for the wheel. 'No! I can!' With a shrug, Lon threw Barry back. Barry gave away about 50 pounds of bulk to the red-haired quarter-wit. The toboggan was careening on and off the path, scraping against the walls of the hedge, sending a flurry of leaves and twigs flying. A branch smacked him in the head and broke off. It read: 'Boy, are you in trouble.'

They were going much, much too fast. Even though the passageway was completely flat, pushing the lever forward magically increased the incline of the slope, increasing the vehicle's speed. Lon had the lever jammed as far forward as it could go.

Barry covered his eyes and prayed. Something zinged past his ear; he looked down and saw that the rivets of a large patch of the floor of the toboggan were popping from the vibration. With every bump (tree root? unlucky squirrel? another drunk?) the sled gave a violent shudder, and the various holes became a little wider.

Lon seemed totally unconcerned, singing his favorite song, 'Do you know the muffin man, the muffin man, the muffin man . . .' Barry spotted something to his right. There, perched on the top of the back seat, was a gremlin, green-skinned, yellow-eyed and chuckling malevolently. He was taking real pleasure in Barry's terror. Leering evilly, he pointed at Barry, then drew a long, talon-like finger across his own throat. The gremlin was predicting the near future, and relishing it. A lot.

'Why, you motherfu—' Barry lunged at him, but just before this book could contain serious profanity, the fragile network of patches holding the sled together gave a final crack, and the toboggan began to separate. Barry grabbed the back of Lon's seat and held on for dear life. Just as his strength began to fail and the contraption was about to fall into two, they slid to a stop in front of a small sign reading, 'Hogsbleede Station.' Chagrined, the gremlin smacked a fist into his palm and disappeared.

'I love to drive,' said Lon. He looked back at Barry, just as the whole back end collapsed. 'Oooh, Barry broke the sled,' he said. Getting out to do a little hopping dance, he pointed and sang, 'Barry broke the sled, Barry broke the sled'

Happy to be alive, Barry crawled queasily over to the exit.

Chapter Four

A VISIT WITH THE
HEAD MASTER

◇◇◇◇◇

The hedgerow dumped them out on Crowley Avenue, Hogsbleede's notorious Strip, a collection of bars, gambling dens, and houses of spectacularly ill-repute that slumped like a police lineup through the middle of that malignant town. Any vice, no matter how nasty, could be satisfied here – for a price. It was a great favorite with the rougher run of Hogwash students, so it was a rare Sunday morning that Hafwid didn't have to make the trek into town to post bail for a motley collection of chewed-up scholar-ruffians. The rumour was that the town jail had a special student section. Barry had always been too scared to find out – and besides, his fans took care of him.

Ahead of them, a clot of Arithromancers, clearly blitzed, were arguing over the future, getting ready to brawl. 'You couldn't predict Christmas if I gave you a calendar, punk!' Hogsbleede was a big convention spot, and no matter how respectable the group was regularly, this burg invariably brought out the worst in them.

'Let's cross the street,' Barry said to Lon, who was mesmerized by the profusion of neon and flashing lights. 'What's "Satyr on Satyr Action" mean?' Lon asked.

'I'll tell you later,' Barry said, stepping over the shards of a broken butterbourbon bottle. Just walking on the Strip made him feel soiled. They finally got to Corleone Street, and took a left. Almost immediately the atmosphere changed from actively evil to simply lawless, and Barry was glad for the improvement. They immediately saw a sign for where Ermine taught, St. Hilary's. This was a good thing, since Barry had twisted his ankle a bit during the toboggan crash.

'Pull down your cap,' he told Lon. 'I can see your hole.'

'Oops,' Lon said. 'My brains get hot.' There was a jingle bell at each of the cap's dual cones, which jingled with every step. It quickly became irritating, but Barry had trained himself to block it out.

Jingle, wince (as pain shot through Barry's ankle), jingle, wince. They turned into a narrow lane, and saw a squat little building, tidy in that compulsive English way, but obviously long past time for demolition. A sign near the door clearly read, 'St. Hilary's Academy for the Marginally-Magical.' The struggling institution had no money for the expensive anti-Muddle spells and enchantments of a place like Hogwash; it relied on the ancient gambit of 'hiding in plain sight.' So far, it had worked – or nobody had cared.

St. Hilary's was one of about a hundred schools, put up in the Fifties, after the Ministry decided that places like Hogwash were snobbish and elitist. Now that house elves did most of the menial jobs, thousands of people were free to aim higher. Every wizard or witch, no matter how talentless or clearly unsuited, deserved magical instruction. It was a noble idea, but in reality such schools were merely underfunded, crumbling holding pens for students destined for a TV-sodden life of obesity and squalor on the dole. St. Hilary's was the most famous of these schools, since a student last year broke into his father's wand cabinet and went postal.

Lon and Barry opened the door and were buffeted by the distinctive perfume of secondary education: a stomach-churning melange of fried food, disinfectant, the too-sweet scents favored by old ladies, and airborne chalk. Taking shallow breaths, Lon and Barry walked down the main hall, and entered a room marked 'Headmaster's Office.'

They were startled to find the disembodied head of a puffy, smoke-haired man levitating some feet about a desk strewn with papers and a large speakerphone. A luxurious pair of muttonchops jutted from both jowls, and acted as hairy aerilons. Behind him was a picture of St. Hilary, the dumpy patron saint of backwards children everywhere.

'. . . but Headmaster, government regulations *require* that the school be free of pixie dust. It causes cancer in rats,' the speaker squawked.

The head swooped down and yelled into the speaker. 'Well, when we start educating rats, I'll be sure to call!' He gave a lusty series of coughs, the kind that pull stuff up from deep down.

'But Headmaster, St. Hilary's is the most infested place we've ever encountered,' the concerned governmental voice said. 'You're putting your students at risk!' Barry thought he would've been quite distinguished-looking, in a porcine way, if he had a body.

'Sir, apparently you haven't heard: here at St. Hilary's, it is the teachers who are at risk. Good day to you!' Coughing violently, the head hung up the phone by slamming its forehead down on the console. The force of this left him momentarily dazed, and he wobbled in the air a little before addressing his visitors.

'Gentlemen – I am Betjeman ffolkes-Ptarmigan,

headmaster of this Godforsaken educational sludgepit.' He had a red mark on his forehead. 'What can I do for you?'

Lon began to speak, but Barry leapt in, since there was no telling what might emerge from that addled half-canine brain.

'Mr. ffolkes-Ptarmigan, we're from Hogwash—'

ffolkes-Ptarmigan's eyes narrowed with immediate cupidity. 'Fine school. What I wouldn't do with just *half* of their budget. A villa on Majorca, perhaps, or a Greek island . . .'

'We're on urgent business for the school. One of your teachers, Ermine Cringer, is a former Hogwesian, and we'd like a word or two with her. If it wouldn't cause too much trouble.'

Barry could see ffolkes-Ptarmigan's mind working – *quid pro quo*, with as much emphasis on the 'quid' as possible.

'Certainly, Mister . . . uh . . .'

'Barry Trotter.' Barry extended his hand. 'And this is my associate, Lon Measly.' Lon waved. 'Hiya!'

'Not *the* Barry Trotter, I trust?'

'Yes, sir.'

The head beamed even more. 'I've read all your books,' ffolkes-Ptarmigan' grin reached alarming proportions as his avarice was well-whetted. 'Such interesting, lucrative adventures you've had. I trust this is your latest one?'

Barry didn't like the way this was going. 'Sort of. I mean, not really. And those books were mostly bullsh—'

ffolkes-Ptarmigan realized he'd overreached. 'Of course. They always are. Now, Ms. Cringer—' The head whipped around to look at the clock on the wall; Barry and Lon got a fine view of his thin, dandruffy backfringe, some of which caught the wind during this brisk pirouette and floated down slowly. How did he comb it? thought Barry. Lon didn't think anything, as was his wont.

'Ms. Cringer is just finishing up her last class of the day, Zoology. It will be over in fifteen minutes.'

'Great – can we wait here?'

ffolkes-Ptarmigan smiled his oily smile. 'No, no, my dear Mr. Trotter, this isn't Hogwash! Just barge right in! In addition to not being very magical, our students aren't very scholarly. They will welcome the interruption.'

The head zoomed over to a bookshelf, grabbed a red binder with his teeth, and yanked it out, sending it to the floor. He descended, opened it, and flicked through its pages with a moist tongue.

'Yet'h thee . . . Ginja . . .' ffolkes-Ptarmigan said as

he flipped. He made a sour face – the ink tasted foul. 'She's in room 207.'

'Oops.' Lon had just broken one of the Headmaster's desk toys, and Barry always took such incidents as a sign to clear out.

'Thanks very much, Mr. ffolkes-Ptarmigan. We'll try not to disturb her class,' Barry said, turning towards the door.

'Don't worry about it,' ffolkes-Ptarmigan said, zooming up to eye level once again. 'Happy to do a favor for the great Barry Trotter. Sure you'd do the same for me, someday.'

Barry reflexively felt for his wallet.

Barry and Lon mounted the stairs, and padded down the hall. Each footfall sent clouds of fine, white dust into the air. Mortar? Plaster? Pixie dust? Unlike the first floor, which simply smelled weird, this one showed that the entire building cried out for immediate demolition, with extreme prejudice.

They peered through the window of Room 207. There was Ermine, in her element, behind a desk, telling other people what to do. In an aggressively dull white blouse, beige skirt and matching corduroy jacket, she stood in front of the most lifeless class Barry had ever seen. The stupidity seemed to come off them in waves.

What was wrong with Ermine's hair? Barry thought. The answer was that an attempt at straightening her unruly locks was growing out, creating an effect that can only be called 'Einsteinian.'

Barry and Lon opened the door silently, waving at Ermine, and slipped into two desks in the back row. Lon was much too big for his, and knocked it over with a clatter. 'Sorry,' he mouthed silently, as every head in the room turned to stare.

'Class, these are two, erm, teachers from another district,' Ermine said. 'They are here for a visit. Proceed, Sally. You were telling us the answer to Question Five,' Ermine said patiently. 'How does a panther repel a dragon?'

An elfin, frizzy-haired blonde girl in a green jumper spoke. 'The panther chases away a dragon by giving a great belch,' Sally said, by rote. 'The dragon cannot stand the smell.'

'Correct, Sally. Who knows the answer to Question Six? Not many of you got this one right. Trevor?'

Barry shuddered inwardly as an insipid Dork boy gave the answer, with a superior smirk. A finer argument for corporal punishment had never graced a classroom.

'Question Six. The dung of which bird is good for eye trouble? Answer: the caladrius.'

I'll stick to my specs, thanks, Barry thought. Lon had given up on trying to force his large body into the desk and was sitting cross-legged on the floor.

'Excellent, Trevor. Thank you.' Ermine glanced at the clock. 'Drat. We're running late, so I'll give the rest of the answers. But before I do, I want to tell you that I was very unhappy with the performance of the class on yesterday's test. All you have to do is read your bestiaries. It's not difficult, nor does it take any magic. But you must apply yourselves – lazy *and* unmagical is no way to go through life.

'Okay, Question Seven: What animal does the lion fear? Answer: the cock.'

Sniggers danced throughout the classroom, including from Lon. Ermine shot him a dirty look.

'Question Eight: How does the hyena lure its prey? Answer: it mimics the sound of human vomiting and sobbing. Question Nine: How do cranes fly in blustery weather? Answer: they eat quantities of sand and small pebbles, to give themselves ballast.'

Barry heard some student mutter, 'Bollocks.' Good for you, he thought.

'Question Ten: How does the beaver avoid capture?

Answer: When pursued by a hunter, it will rip off its testicles, and hurl them at his assailant.'

A student said, 'Trevor's already done it,' and several others laughed.

Ermine tapped her ruler on the lectern. 'That's *enough*.' Barry recognized the last-gasp efforts of a young teacher to keep control in those giddy moments before the bell rings. 'Just because we have guests, that's no reason to act up!'

Suddenly the class exploded in laughter. Some of them pointed at Ermine, who looked down. A student had made her shirt invisible.

'Well, aren't we clever, misusing our paltry knowledge as usual. Take a good long look, Mr. Palaver – you're going to pay for it, you might as well get your money's worth.' Faced with their teacher's nakedness, some students blushed. However, a few shadow-jowled boys looked unashamedly, appraisingly, and Barry felt bad for Ermine, having to deal with such a jaded bunch. She ejected the student with businesslike aplomb.

Her shirt slowly faded back into view. 'Now, for the extra credit question – and since none of you got it, I'll have to read it myself: Everybody knows about the jaculus, a flying snake that throws itself at its prey like a javelin . . .'

A hand shot up. 'It's like a spear.' The hand dropped.

'Yes, but wait to be called on, Murphy. Now, for extra credit, name two other interesting facts about serpents. Obviously, there could be any number of these, but a few are: before drinking water, snakes spew their venom into a hole; a snake will never attack a naked man; if a snake goes blind, it can cure itself by eating fennel; if a snake drinks the spit of a fasting man, it dies; and finally, there is a type of two-headed snake that can roll like a hoop.'

The bell rang. Ermine shouted over the class, 'Read the section on Fish for tomorrow.' There was a groan. 'There will be a quiz.' There was a bigger groan, and Ermine walked over to Barry and Lon.

'I saw a hoop snake once,' Lon told her excitedly.

'No, you didn't, Lon,' Ermine said. 'To what do I owe this hideous intrusion, I mean, unexpected pleasure? If this is about being on "Behind the Magic," the answer is still "no."'

'Nice to see you, too, Ermine,' Barry said. 'It's kind of a long story. Is there someplace we can go to talk?'

'The last time you said that to me, Barry Trotter, I ended up with a ripped blouse and shoes that smelled like vomit.'

'I don't remember that,' Barry said.

'I'm not surprised, Mr. Purple Jesus Punch,' Ermine said with a sigh. 'Follow me. We'll go to the lounge.'

Moments later, the three were sitting in uncomfortable plastic chairs, in a smoky, dingy room. Is there anything more depressing than hackneyed motivational posters? If so, Barry didn't want to know.

'Coffee?' Ermine asked, brandishing a pot. Nobody accepted; she poured herself a Styrofoam cup full of acrid sludge the consistency of maple syrup. 'I'm an addict,' Ermine said cheerfully, acknowledging that anyone who would willingly drink what she had just poured herself really was a slave to the Demon Bean. She put the pot back, then tapped the side of her cup with her wand. It lightened a few creams' worth. She sipped and Barry massaged his ankle, which was feeling better. Lon was drawing his name in a pile of sugar.

'So what's up? Is He-Who-Smells acting up again?' Ermine asked.

'Nah, Valumart has nothing to do with this,' Barry said. 'Or maybe he does, I don't know.'

After he had explained the situation, Ermine stirred her cup of muck a bit and said, 'So you want my help?'

'Yes! Lon's nice and all – loyal – but, well, you know. A crow could beat him in Scrabble.'

Ermine said, 'I'm to be the brains of the operation, is that it?' Smiling, she calculated a bit. 'Actually, I do have some vacation days. I may regret this – I always do – but what the hell.'

Relieved, Barry said, 'That's great, Ermine! It'll be just like old times!'

Ermine smiled a little less. 'Not quite, Barry. Not everybody is a brand name adored by millions, you know. Some of us have to work for a living.'

Barry was in a familiar bind. He wanted to explain that he didn't have any money, that he'd just gotten a bit at the beginning and a little more every time he talked to the author. Oh, and there were the endorsements, but those got cancelled after a Valumartian acne attack.[6] Still, his pride liked being considered a rich guy.

'My price is, pay off my student loans,' Ermine said. 'My parents work for the National Health, and I need all the money I can get.' Ermine's parents were holistic dentists, and the pickings are slim for dentists who 'refuse to remove the tooth from its natural ecosystem.'

Picking up the spirit, Lon chimed in. 'Yeah, Barry, I want *five bucks*!' He was ignored.

---

[6] For details, see the fourth book in the series, *Barry Trotter and the Acne of Fire*.

Barry panicked, 'But Ermine, I don't—'

'Then I can't.'

'Be reasonable, Ermine.'

'I am being reasonable, Barry.' She cracked each knuckle slowly; Barry recognized this gesture from many earlier times when Ermine had somebody – usually Barry – by the man-grapes, and was squeezing. 'Okay, okay.'

'Got a plan?'

'Don't I always?' Barry said. 'We're going to kidnap J.G. Rollins, and hide her someplace. If they don't stop the movie, we'll turn her into guacamole.'

Ermine made a face. 'That's a little bloody-minded, don't you think? J.G. has always struck me as a reasonable sort, so let's just find her and ask her nicely.'

'And if she doesn't agree?'

'Then we kidnap her.' Ermine said, 'But there'll be no guacamoling. That's just as bad as Lord Valumart.'

Ermine raised her glass to drink. Suddenly, she screamed, throwing the cup to the floor.

'What?' Barry and Lon exclaimed, as Ermine ran around the room spitting and wiping her mouth furiously. She pointed at the coffee cup. She gave a gag, and sprinted out of the room as fast as her sensible shoes could carry her.

The boys looked down into the Styrofoam cup, and saw . . . an ear, so pallid and desiccated it must've come from a corpse. Not only was the coffee undrinkable, it was full of Dork Magic! And now, somebody knew their plan. Angrily, Barry grabbed the cup and yelled into it. 'Go tell Lord Valumart he smells like bad Chinese food!' Then he poured it down the sink.

Chapter Five

THE RIGHT SNUFF

෧෩෩

As the trio left the school, Barry said to Ermine, 'So, what do you think the best way to get to Scotland is? Shall we take the Magic Bus?'

'Ugh,' Ermine said. She had an aversion to Magic Buses. For one thing, since her parents were Muddles, she had to sit in the back. 'The last time I rode in one of those, Keith Moon's ghost spilled cheap plonk all over me. It stank so bad, I had to burn my dress.'

'All right, then. Should we use a little Muddle magic?' Barry asked, sticking out his thumb.

'Can we do the hedgerows again?' Lon pleaded. '*Please?*'

'No!' Barry said. His bowels gave a heave at the mere mention of it.

'Hold on a moment.' Ermine rooted around in her handbag, a cute little red number. 'Aha,' she said, and pulled out a flat metal tin about the size of her palm. 'Travelling snuff.'

'Can you get a buzz off it?' Barry asked.

Ermine made a face at Barry. 'Shut up, mini-mind. It's a way to travel long-distances without "misting off."' Evaporating and disevaporating (vulgarly called 'misting off') were how wizards and witches got from place to place, riding the breeze as sentient puffs of damp – once they had received their license, of course. Lon had long since turned sixteen, but that murky dog brain of his made the Department of Evaporation Services wary. Barry thought that was terribly unfair; all Lon might do was chase a few cars. But evaporating without a license was a hefty ticket, so 'misting off' was out.

'It works like this: you sniff some into your nose, and – you know how, when you sneeze, the stuff comes shooting out your nose at a bazillion miles an hour?'

'Yeah.'

'With travelling snuff, the stuff stands still but *you* shoot out!'

'Cool!' said Lon, reaching for the silver tin.

Ermine deftly blocked him. 'Wait, Lon. First, take off your socks.'

'Huh?' Barry said.

'Just do it, okay?' Lon grabbed the back of his collar

and began to pull. 'No, Lon. Not your shirt – your socks.' Barry and Lon sat on the ground untying their shoes (Lon's were velcro), peeling off their socks. Ermine stood above them, looking smugly efficient. Barry had forgotten how much he didn't like being bossed by her.

'Give them to me. Gad, Barry, ever heard of laundry? These could stand by themselves. Now stand next to each other. Stick out your left arm, Lon. Barry, your right.' She took a sock and tied their wrists together. 'Now, your feet.'

Once they were attached, she slid next to Lon and tied herself to his free hand and foot. 'This is so we don't go flying away from each other. Which way is Scotland?'

'That way, I think,' Barry said. They galumphed 90 degrees to the left.

'Oh, I almost forgot.' Ermine pulled out a pair of sunglasses from her purse and put them on. They were a wedge-shaped piece of smoked brown plastic, real old-lady glasses. Barry gave a derisive snort.

'Laugh all you want, nimrod,' Ermine said. 'These MagiSpex will let me see where J.G. Rollins' mansion is. I got 'em at Seers.

'Everybody ready? Take a handful. Remember,

when we start to descend, jam some more up in there. Ready, set – *sniff!'*

Lon sneezed first, and shot into the air, yanking the others skyward. Barry's arm felt like it was being dislocated. Then he sneezed and found that pulling was much more comfortable than being pulled. The air was a little chilly; at least it wasn't raining.

After a few sneezes, they were a good distance up, and could see a panoply of lawbreaking and squalor beneath them. The school was in a frightfully crappy neighbourhood. Three kids were setting fire to an abandoned sofa. A robber stopped breaking into a car to gawp. A housewife snapped a photo from her back door. Barry made a face to spite her, and she flipped him off. Finally, Ermine's schnozz kicked in, and the figures receded.

The trio cruised along, falling into a rhythm: Barry and Lon sneezing heavily to provide the power, Ermine sneezing more frequently, almost daintily, nudging them this way and that whenever necessary, like retrorockets on a space capsule.

Lon was first to see it: off in the distance, two dragons, Irish Whiskeybreaths, were playing a game with an airliner. The dragons were flapping beside the jet filled with Muddles, each no doubt vacillating between their old reliable disbelief, and trousers-fouling terror. The dragons were breathing fire on the fuselage, each one trying to see how hot they could make the plane without igniting the fuel.

They watched this game for several minutes, with the plane desperately trying to evade the dragons and the dragons effortlessly maintaining their positions, until Barry decided he'd had enough and fished out his wand. Timing it between sneezes, Barry yelled,

'*Cumulus!*'

The dragons immediately turned into puffy, white versions of their former selves. They looked about puzzledly for a moment, then dissipated.

They ought to be getting close now. Using her old lady glasses, Ermine peered down through the clouds for the fabulous Rollins estate. Eventually, she pointed earthward and nodded 'yes.' Lon was about to give them another mighty blast, but in the nick of time, Barry reached his free hand over under Lon's nostrils. For one horrible second, he wondered if a blocked sneeze would blow Lon's head off. It didn't, but twin jets of air shot through his head-holes, flapping the flaps of his hat so fast they were a blur. Laughing, they floated like leaves to the sand below, with Barry's slowly dissipating sock musk as their stinky contrail.

Ermine and Barry started untying themselves. 'What do you think of travelling snuff?' Ermine asked.

'It's better than the tube,' Barry said. 'Hard on your sinuses, though.' He felt his face, which was warming up, and starting to hurt like hell. 'Mine feel like I buffed them with sandpaper.'

'Well, at least we didn't have to worry about climbing the gate,' Ermine said, pointing to the massive wrought iron fence. On their side of it was a strip of beach 25 yards deep, bordered by impossibly blue water. On the other was the dewy, damp greenness of Scotland.

Something white at the base of the fence caught Ermine's eye. 'Look, it's a rabbit!' she cried. The placement of a Caribbean beach in the middle of Scotland was clearly perplexing to this, and doubtless many other, indigenous creatures. 'He's caught.'

'I will save him! Woof!' Lon said, and bounded off. The others followed.

The rabbit had wedged itself between two posts (wands shooting fire, Barry noticed). Lon gripped them at shoulder level, testing their strength; it was a queer feeling – the beach side of the metal was painfully hot, but the fen side was chilly. He tugged, but they weren't budging.

'Looks like I'll have to use – this,' Lon said, pulling

out his wand. It was covered with puffy stickers featuring Timothy the Treacle Train and Bradley the Puce-Colored Dinosaur.

'I don't think that's a very good idea,' said Barry. The path of well-meaning destruction that Lon and his wand had carved out over the years was considerable. 'Maybe you should . . .'

Lon paid no attention, and knelt down. The rabbit was vibrating with terror, its red eyes wide and rolling. 'Nice bunny, I'll get you out. Pretty bun . . . YOW!' The terrified animal had nipped Lon's finger. 'Arrgh!' Lon yelled, popping his finger in his mouth. 'You farthead!' Lon pointed his wand at the rabbit, and a red beam immediately turned it into jerky. Then, realizing what he had just done, Lon burst into tears.

Ermine tried to comfort him. 'There, there, Lon. Don't cry.'

'Come on, you two,' Barry said impatiently. 'It's hot out here.'

'Yeah,' Lon sniffed, his tears subsiding. 'Can I take off my hat?'

'No – oh, wait,' Ermine rooted around once more, and pulled out a rubber bathing cap. 'Yes, wear this if you like. I was going to do water aerobics this afternoon, before you two shanghai'ed me.'

'Thanks,' Lon said. Barry wasn't so sure if that was

the right response, since the frilly white latex cap looked even more ridiculous on him than what it replaced.

'Hey Erm, what's with this place? It doesn't look like Scotland to me.'

'Yes, well, when J.G. first hit it big, y'see, she paid some wizard landscapers to carve out a little Caribbean hideaway for her. They did it in exchange for frequent mentions in the next book. Now they make a packet doing mini-versions of the Rollins estate for fans.' Ermine stood up and brushed the sand off her backside. 'So many, in fact, that's it's starting to cause global warming. It was all over the newspapers.'

'The newspapers are all lies,' Barry said. 'It's what the corporations want you to think.'

Ermine made a dismissive sound with her lips. 'You've been saying that since you were fifteen, and it was simple-minded then, you poser.'

Barry was crafting a rejoinder that would finally teach Ermine the way the world really worked, when he saw a group of humans clumped together, on the beach ahead. 'Let's ask these guys where the Rollins' castle is,' Barry said.

'Good idea,' Ermine agreed.

As they got closer, the identity of the group became clear: it was a chain-gang of Earth Eaters. The incarcerated followers of Lord Valumart were being overseen by a paunchy wizard-cop in mirrored sunglasses who spat tobacco and swore at them, holding back a slavering, sixteen-headed dog.

'Y'all better keep eatin', else Fifi here might just slip outen mah hand,' the wizard guard said. 'Y'all don't want that, do you?'

'Mnfhth,' chorused the Earth Eaters. Each of them was busily chewing rocks, and spitting the result, fine-grained said, on to the beach. The Ministry of Magical Corrections had landed a lucrative contract to widen J.G.'s beach.

'Excuse me, officer,' Ermine said. 'Could you direct us to the Rollins estate?' Several of the hellhound's heads – those that weren't nipping each other's ears – tried to sniff Lon's bottom. Lon reciprocated.

One of the prisoners recognized Barry, and threw himself at him. 'Mr. Trotter, you gotta help me! I was framed!' His breath smelled like dirt, and with each word, a little grit landed on Barry's face.

The cop pulled the hapless wizard off with one pudgy hand. 'Get back ter chawin', amigo,' he drawled. 'It's ovuh theah, Miss,' the cop said to Ermine, gesturing in a strange way. 'I'd ask y'all whut ch'all was doin' here, but seeing as it's the great Barry Trotter un'all . . .'

After the cop's spell, an impressive cluster of stucco and tile buildings was suddenly visible off in the distance. 'Thanks, officer,' Ermine said, and they trudged off in that direction, Lon gallumphing ahead.

As they walked, Barry attempted to make small talk. 'How's teaching duds? Do you like it?'

Ermine sniffed, 'The proper term is "marginally-magical".' Barry decided he'd already heard enough on the topic, but Ermine continued. 'Marginally-magical Muddles play a vital role in our economy, especially the rapidly growing service industries. St. Hilary's allows them to acquire the knowledge and skills that they need to get real, satisfying jobs. Twenty years ago, the only thing they could do was eke out a few bucks as beauticians or conjurers at children's birthday parties. Now, they can live with dignity.'

Listening to Ermine was often like watching cable television, and not one of the more interesting channels. 'Thank you, Mother Theresa. Look, Lon's almost to the door; let's catch up. I'll race you!' A pound of sand in each shoe later, Barry and Ermine joined Lon in front of a medium-sized house, made of stucco and roofed with thatch.

'Doesn't seem rich enough,' Barry said. 'I thought she was loaded.'

Chapter Five

'Can I knock?' Lon said excitedly.

'Use the knocker,' said Ermine. There was a brass, fist-shaped knocker hanging on the door. As soon as Lon touched it, a doorbell chimed.

'Ooh, it's magical,' Ermine said.

'Ooh, it's stupid,' Barry retorted.

A moment later, the door opened, and a tall man in a three-piece suit stood in front of them.

'Can I help you?' he intoned pompously, raising a pair of thick, black eyebrows. Barry noted that he had liver spots on his forehead, and began to count them.

'We're here to see Ms. Rollins? Is she in?' Ermine said.

'Is she expecting you?' the butler said. His eyebrows reminded Barry of caterpillars.

'Um, no.' The door began to close slightly. 'But it's very important that we talk to her.' The door closed faster. 'We're fans of her books —'

The door was only open a crack now, and Ermine was desperate. 'This is Barry Trotter!' she blurted out, pushing Barry forward. He hit the nearly-closed door with a clunk. 'Hey! That was my head!'

Immediately, the door swung open. 'A thousand pardons. Come right in; let me show you to the living room.'

'Thanks,' Ermine said, a bit irritated by the way

Barry's name had gotten results. She began to take off her shoes.

'Wait a tick – we don't want to track sand in.'

The butler gave a wave of his hand. 'No matter – it's magical. It will melt away by itself.'

Twenty-two spots, Barry thought. I hope I die before I get horrible-looking. Did the butler's eyebrows just move? They *were* caterpillars!

They were led into a room that looked like the entrance hall of an ancestral castle. Ermine paused halfway over the threshold, looking at the modest stucco outside and then marveling at the immensely bigger, Ye Olde Tyme Manor structure inside. 'Come on,' Barry whispered, 'Act like you've seen magic before.' She always turned pure Muddle in situations like this.

They followed the butler down a wide hallway. He scooped the caterpillar off his brow and put it in his coat pocket. Everywhere there was dark wood, rich tapestries, old, gloomy, paintings of old, pale people. It looked a lot like Hogwash would, Barry thought, if it hadn't been tormented by the constant rain of petty destruction that is the calling card of students everywhere.

The butler opened a door into what appeared to be the Great Hall; flags hung from sconces in the walls, each showing the Rollins' family crest: a lion and a unicorn rampant, on a field of gold, with a screw and an eightball framing the motto, '*Semper ubi sub ubi.*'

'Wait here,' the butler said. 'I will get the gentleman of the house.'

Gentleman? 'Thank you,' Ermine said, and gave a little curtsy. Barry elbowed her. The butler said nothing and left.

'Ass!' Barry hissed at Ermine. 'He's just the butler!'

Lon had wandered down to the opposite end of the room, which was dominated by a huge fireplace. They went down to investigate, and stretch out on the large, leather couch.

A heatless green-and-blue fire crackled merrily. Silverfish colors, Barry noted. He saw a small dial on the side of the grate, with settings like 'cool,' 'warm,' 'hot,' 'infernal,' and 'you cannot be serious.' It was set on 'cool'; he cranked it up to 'hot.' An enormous blast of warmth came from the fire.

'Hey,' Lon said, looking up from a snowglobe he had found. 'You're gonna make me sweat in Ermine's hat!'

'Ick!' said Ermine. 'Barry, turn it down.'

Grinning evilly, Barry was just about to turn it up to 'infernal' when his interrobang throbbed. He looked up, and there, standing at the far end of the room was an all-too-familiar figure. The gleaming, spike-topped helmet; the impossibly bushy moustache; the chestful of made-up medals; the glittering, porcine eyes pressed like twin black fruitgums into ten pounds of lard ...

'Ve meet again, Trotter. Prepare to die.'

Chapter Six

THE PINEWOOD
PECKERWOOD

⟨∞⟩

The trio sprang into action. Ermine fell into her characteristic battle crouch, which made her look like a Shaolin master suffering from severe menstrual cramps. She clutched her stomach and mumbled furiously, the spit flying as her hex took shape. It winged towards Lord Valumart, hitting him square in the stomach.

'Oof,' said the Dork Lord.

Lon threw the snowglobe blindly and leapt behind the couch. It landed with a tinkle nowhere near Valumart, but this bought Barry the time he needed to extract his wand. Strapped to his inner thigh, it was sweaty and disgusting, but there was no time to wipe it now. Barry yelled, 'Aveda Neutrogena!' In an instant, the infamous death-by-moisturizing spell spurted forth in a bolt of viscous green fire.

Lord Valumart screamed, his voice somewhat

higher-pitched than Barry remembered it. The Dork Lord skittered behind the door. An instant later, the green bolt hit it with a loud, wet smack, turning it into a slab of aloe-smelling goo.

As the goo slid to the floor the three saw something that they never thought possible: the great Lord Valumart on his knees, with his hands up, yelling, 'Truce! Uncle! Please stop! I was only kidding!'

Huh? He couldn't be giving up, Barry thought – there's plenty of book left. The bespectacled heartthrob of the wizarding world approached, warily, wand out. Ermine followed, still in a half-crouch, ready to hex again if necessary. Lon peeped over the couch.

'Hey Dork Lord,' Barry said. 'Not so tough without all your mud-mouthed cronies, eh?'

'Yeah,' said Ermine, piling on. 'I bet you're about to nip off your testicles and throw them at us!' Sometimes her great intelligence got in the way of Ermine's sense of humor.

As they came closer, they saw that Valumart's cadaver-like skin seemed to be smudged, and that the spiky helmet covered a mop of blond hair.

Barry grabbed it: 'Valumart, I've been meaning to tell you this for years: that has got to be the *worst* hairpiece I've ever seen.' He gave it a yank, but it didn't budge.

Chapter Six

'Ow! OW! Stop it, you bully.' Valumart grabbed Barry's hand, trying to lessen the pulling, 'I'm not really Valumart—'

'What?' said Ermine.

'I just do that to scare off the fans! You have no idea how many of them there are—'

'Oh, I think I know,' Barry said wearily, letting go. If he had sixpence for every faux-Valumart he'd beaten over the years . . . 'Who are you?'

The man scrambled to his feet. He pulled off his moustache, and threw the ends into his upturned helmet.

'Hold still for a second,' said Ermine, now out of battle crouch. 'I have to remove the constipation hex I put on you. Now, what's the remedy for a Bowel Blocker . . . ?'

Upright, the man gained some dignity. Brushing the dust off, he said, 'My name is Trevor Nunnally. I am Ms. Rollins' live-in companion. How do you do?' Each of them shook the proffered hand. 'Normally, I'd sic the dogs on you, but if it's really the great Barry' – Barry raised his wand menacingly, and Nunnally flinched – 'which it so clearly *is*, there can be no doubt of that, you'll all have to stay for dinner. Will you?'

Given the reception they had just received, Barry

was inclined to say no. 'Yes,' said Ermine. 'We'd be delighted.'

Barry started to sheath his wand, then licked his thumb and rubbed it. No luck; the Led Zeppelin ZOSO runes he had drawn on with a Sharpie when he was 14 didn't budge. He was such an idiot back then. Trevor was staring at it, so he put it away quickly.

'I'm hungry!' said Lon.

'All right, we'll stay,' Barry said.

'Excellent. I'll summon the cook,' said Nunnally. He removed a small silver bell from his pocket, and rang it. Almost instantly, a familiar creature flitted into the room. He was small, dark, perhaps Spanish, with bugged-out eyes and an incredibly pointy moustache.

'You rrrrang, Mast— BARRRRY! It is the gret Barrrry Trrotter!' Dali the house-elf sprang into Barry's arms, still rolling the final r. 'I aming so happy to see you!' He kissed Barry on both cheeks Continental-style, his moustache coming perilously close to going up Barry's nostril.

'I'm happy to see you, too, Dali. You owe me some money.'

'Oh, Misterr Barrry, I always meaning to rrrepay to you those *pesetas*. You are having them beforrre *esta noche*. Arrre you staying herrre long?' The profusion of Latin rolled 'r's – which Barry could never do, and

Chapter Six

suspected that Dali talked this way to twit him – made conversations with Dali take forrreverrr.

Nunnally tapped Dali on the shoulder. 'If I might, I'd like to talk about dinner.' Dali dropped from Barry's arms, and whipped out a small notepad. 'I arrre rrready,' he said.

'Tonight, Dali, we shall have a feast in honour of our guests. I will leave the details of the menu to you,' Nunnally said. 'But spare no expense. And bring something special up from the cellar.'

'How lovely,' said Ermine sweetly. Barry could tell that she was falling for him. It happened once or twice an adventure, guaranteed if the guy was a creep. Barry was resigned to it.

'You can depend on me, sirrr,' Dali said, slipping the notepad into his pocket. 'I aming to prrreparrre it immediately.' He twirled his moustache, popped his eyes, and skittered away.

Nunnally turned to his guests. 'Would you all excuse me for a few moments? I need to get out of this ridiculous costume.' He was right; the white pancake was now all over his jingling tunic, and the cape was covered with dust from his cowering, punctuated by flecks of the deadly lotion. Barry saw that the red satin lining of the cape was frayed and ripping.

Nunnally looked about him. 'Drippings?' The liver-spotted butler emerged from the shadows, where he had been stroking his caterpillars. 'Show our guests to the dining room. I shall be there shortly.'

Barry, Lon and Ermine followed Drippings through a wood-panelled maze of halls to the dining room. It was huge, with walls of red fabric and gilt-edged paintings packed together cheek by jowl. It was a little over the top, frankly. I should have asked her for more money, Barry thought.

'That's a Turner,' Ermine said, pointing at an expensive seascape.

'Did he mean for it to be so blurry?' said Lon.

The room was dominated by a long table, covered with spotless linen and interspersed with golden candelabras, with space for 40, at least. The three felt foolish, cramming themselves down at one end. Barry said to Lon, jokingly, 'Why don't you sit down there?'

'Okay,' Lon said cheerfully. Barry started to tell him that it was a joke, but decided not to.

Presently, Nunnally appeared, and sat at the end of the table, between Barry and Ermine. 'Why's he all the way down there?' he said, pointing towards Lon.

'He rolled in raccoon poo,' Barry said *sotto voce*. Nunnally was puzzled but didn't pursue it. Lon smiled and waved, and went back to driving his silverware around the table, complete with sputtering, spitty car sounds.

As they waited for Dali to present dinner, they talked. Nunnally was very interested in Lord Valumart, 'to improve my impression.'

'But why do you do an impression?' Ermine asked.

'Let's just say it plays a role in J.G.'s and my relationship,' Nunnally said, blushing slightly. 'So you've actually *seen* He-Who-Smells?'

'Who, Lon?' Barry said. 'Oh, Valumart. Yeah.'

'Well . . . what does he smell like?'

Barry paused, trying to conjure the distinctive odor of Ultimate Evil in his nostrils. 'The closest I can come to it is toejam. He tries to cover it up with cologne, which only makes it smell like spicy toejam.' Barry turned to Ermine. 'It's that dimestore stuff. I always forget the name of it.'

'Bold Spice,' Ermine said, keeping her eyes fixed on Nunnally. 'It's a knock-off.'

'You're kidding me? A man that rich and powerful wears Bold Spice?'

'Yeah, well, Lord V.'s kind of . . . peculiar.'

'I'm hungry!' Lon yelled at them. Their host reached into his pocket, pulled out a small box, and threw it to Lon. Lon caught it.

'Raisins!' Lon chirped. 'Boy, if the rest of this dinner is as good as this, well, it's gonna be pretty good!'

'You were saying.'

'I forgot what—'

'You were telling Trevor how He-Who-Smells is a weirdo,' Ermine said.

It was 'Trevor,' eh? Ermine was right on schedule, Barry thought.

Nunnally turned serious. 'So Barry, in your opinion – what makes He-Who-Smells so evil?'

'Nobody really knows,' Barry said. 'Though he got teased constantly when he was at Hogwash. There is a rumor—' he turned to Ermine, 'Should I tell him the rumor?'

'Yes, please!' Nunnally said.

Ermine looked put out. 'If you must.'

An unkind smile crept onto Barry's face. 'Well, some people say that the great Lord Valumart was the victim of a botched circumcision.'

'No!' Nunnally was genuinely shocked.

'Yeah! Isn't that amazing?' They all snickered.

'What are you guys talking about?' Lon yelled.

'The surgeon was drunk,' Ermine chimed in.

'A guy who went to Hogwash with him told me that he's all colors of the rainbow,' Barry said.

Wait 'til I put that up on the website!' Nunnally said with glee.

'I'm still hungry!' Lon shouted irritably. He wore his napkin like a bib, and banged his silverware on the table. His Hogwash friends were familiar with this mood. 'I see "King Baby" has emerged,' Ermine said.

Then Dali appeared, followed by a troop of house-elves carrying covered silver salvers. 'Yay!' Lon yelled, from the end of the room.

'Lady and gentlemen, I prrresent to you, my latest masterrrpiece!' On Dali's signal, the elves uncovered the plates. The famished humans saw plates filled with twisted copper wire, clockwork gears, Styrofoam peanuts; a tureen of paint, and – clearly the *piece de resistance* – a silver platter heaped with liquid plaster-of-Paris. Barry's mouth fell open – *this* was dinner?

'Amazing, isn't it?' Nunnally said, misreading Barry's horror as admiration. 'Thank you, Dali, you've truly outdone yourself tonight.'

'Thank you, masterrr,' Dali said, bowing low.

A house elf led a mammoth red gelatin into the room, cracking an enormous bullwhip and swearing loudly. The gelatin, which had eyeballs, ears, and other biological necessities embedded in it, shambled slowly forward, leaving a presumably cherry-flavored trail of slime in its wake. The blob quivered whenever the whip was raised.

'Why on Earth did you bring that up here?' Nunnally said.

'Because you asked for something special from the cellar,' Dali said. 'I naturally assumed you meant Clarence.'

'No, no! I meant wine. Clarence has been in J.G.'s family for generations,' Nunnally explained to the table. 'It wouldn't be right to eat him.'

'My mistake. I shall rreturrn him to his quarrrterrrs. Bon appetit,' Dali said, and left the room.

'Dali is the foremost surrealist cook in the United Kingdom, and maybe the world,' Nunnally said, beaming. 'There aren't many of them. Dig in, everybody.'

'How?' Barry said as Ermine dutifully loaded up her plate with inedible flotsam and jetsam.

'Hey! Send some of that stuff down here!' said Lon.

'Okay, but you're not going to like it,' said Ermine, picking up the plate of plaster and bringing it to him. 'Wow, that's heavy.'

'What I like to do with Dali's creations is arrange them on my plate. Some patterns I create are pleasing; others confrontational; others strangely sad somehow.

Meanwhile—' he pulled several more boxes of raisins out of his pocket. 'I find these very filling.'

Barry took it without relish. 'Thanks.'

Apparently feeling that there was now a bond between them, Nunnally's mien turned serious. 'Barry, I have to be honest: I think the books are silly rubbish, but they do have their uses. For one thing, it makes life a lot easier for Muddles who are magical but don't know it yet.'

'How?' Ermine asked, smiling sweetly. Barry's gorge rose.

'Say you're 11, and you discover you're magical – if you've read the series, chances are you won't freak out. Oh, you may be disappointed when you find out that the real wizard life isn't nearly as fun or glamorous as J.G.'s books, but that's a small thing.

'I remember when I discovered I was a wizard,' Nunnally said. 'I started hearing my pet gecko talking to herself. "I am going to lick my eyeball. There, I just licked my own eyeball."'

'You're a pretzeltongue?' Barry said.

'Yes. I thought I was going insane. Luckily I lived next door to a weird woman who took me under her wing, a Mrs. Robinson,' Nunnally looked wistful. 'She taught me the ways of the wizarding world.'

Ermine's face fell; Nunnally didn't notice. 'Still – I

wish those books were around when I was a kid. It would've made coming out of the magical closet a lot easier. There used to be an appalling number of magical Muddles going 'round the bend. Now they just smile to themselves and wait for the acceptance letter from Hogwash to arrive.'

Nunnally gestured expansively with a raisin. 'Why, if Barry Trotter had been around, maybe William Shakespeare would've become a profitable member of society.'

Ermine snorted into her plate of Styrofoam peanuts, blowing several into the air. 'But—'

Nunnally paid no attention, mesmerized by the sound of his own voice. 'Anyway, J.G. is getting tired of them. Has she told you?'

'Told me what?' Barry asked.

Nunnally paused. 'Hell, this is awkward. I assumed she had told you.'

'Spit it out, for God's sake,' Barry said, irritated.

'This will be the last Barry Trotter book, I'm afraid.'

'What?' they chorused.

'I probably shouldn't tell you this, but J.G. has let me in on a little secret: you die in this one, Barry.'

'But why would she . . . she can't . . .' A chill went through Barry's body as he saw his notoriety ebbing away.

'Well, you're an adult now. Your adventures are no longer appropriate; what is she going to write, *Barry Trotter and the Difficult Tax Return*? Or maybe she's just sick of it – I don't know, you'd have to ask her. But I do know she's planning to hang up her pen.' He looked over at Barry, with an amused expression that showed he didn't share the general consternation that wreathed the table. 'Don't worry, Barry – you may die, but you won't feel a thing.'

Nunnally pushed away his plate. 'Well. Wasn't that nice?' He looked at his watch. 'It's getting a bit late. Do you all need to be moving on? Where were you going, anyway?' He laughed, possibly at this book's inept plotting. 'I just realized, I still have no idea why you're here.'

Hungry and tired, Barry said crossly, 'We're looking for J.G.'

Lon leapt in. 'We're going to kidna—'

'—talk to her.' Ermine said, saving the day. 'We want to convince her to stop the Barry Trotter movie.'

'Oh, J.G. has nothing to do with that. If I were you, I'd go talk to Fantastic Books in New York – they own all the rights. But why would you lot want to *stop* the movie? I'd think it was a dream come true.'

Ermine said, 'It's rather complicated, but let's just

say that if the movie comes out, Barry will have to grow up and get a real job.'

Nunnally gave a guffaw. 'Oooh, I feel your pain. Life's too short for a real job. I myself have been fortunate enough – through J.G.'s generosity – to devote the last several years of my life to something that I believe can change the world.' Nunnally's face lit up. 'Can I show you? Would you like to see it?'

'Oh, yes, please!' Ermine gushed. Barry was amused to find that the inedible surrealist supper hadn't cooled her eternally-questing libido.

'Right, follow me.' Nunnally got up, and practically trotted out of the room. Barry, Ermine and Lon followed.

They reached a door. Nunnally stood in front of it and asked them gravely, 'If I show you what's behind this door, do you promise not to steal my idea? I'd usually make you sign something, but I guess I'll simply have to trust you.' Nunnally opened the door, flipping on the lights. Twenty fluorescent fixtures buzzed to life, revealing a row of 144 wood tracks, all humped at one end, and sloping gradually down to the floor.

'This is it,' Nunnally said proudly.

'This is what?' Barry asked.

'Oh, nothing much. Only the way to end all conflict in the world, for all time.'

The trio looked on dumbly.

'It's pinewood derby! See, look!' Nunnally walked over to a large chest, opened it, and pulled out two wheeled objects. When his back was turned, Barry looked at Ermine and made the 'cuckoo' sign and pointed at their host. Ermine frowned and hit him on the upper arm. It hurt.

'Here you go, Barry, you take Trinidad.' It was a wedge-shaped piece of wood, painted in the green, blue and yellow of that Caribbean nation. He flicked the right front wheel, spinning it. 'Ermine, use this one – Great Britain. It's the one I always use.'

'Thank you,' she said.

'Ermine, Barry: put your cars next to each other, at the top of the track. When I say, 'go,' let them roll.'

'You're going down, Trotter!' Ermine said to Barry, running her wedge-shaped car back and forth on the track aggressively.

'*Go!*'

The two contestants let go. Sure enough, Barry lost – Ermine's car reached the finish line about a second before his, which seemed to have a wobble.

'Let me try!' Lon cried. Nunnally gave him a car from the chest. 'Wasn't that fun?'

'Sure,' said Barry. 'But I don't get how it can save the world.' Nunnally wasn't barking mad, yet, but he was definitely growling.

Their addlepated host swept his arm across the room. 'In this chamber, there are 144 tracks; one for each sovereign nation in the world. Currently, they all sit in New York, at the UN, debating about how to solve this or that problem. But, you see, logic and argument have their drawbacks. Words can be slippery, agreements can be confusing. Things don't always mean what you think they mean, especially if you're a little dim. This method is much fairer. As I always say, "The cars never lie."'

Barry wasn't convinced. 'But why cars? Why not, say, badminton?'

Nunnally was appalled. 'My God, that would be anarchy!'

Seeing that Barry wasn't convinced, the crane-like man pulled out an extremely dog-eared piece of paper, and, reprising a performance given innumerable times in front of his bedroom mirror, read:

'Only through racing can the world's problems truly be solved. Only through the mute judgment of aerodynamics and gravity – through impartial, cleansing speed – can we find our way to Truth's Finish Line. Because, if you look at it a certain way, isn't life itself a race? And is it mere coincidence that we're called the human *race*? Aren't we all just small, wooden cars, hurtling down a wooden track the size of Infinity?'

'But—'

'Go ahead, call me a racist. That doesn't mean I'm not *right*.'

It doesn't mean you're not mad as a hatter, Barry thought.

As crazy as his plan sounded – *was* – Barry suspected that Nunnally would be successful; after all, he had an enormous melon of a head. One thing that Barry had learned from his hobnobbing with the rich and famous (not as often as he'd liked, sure, but still, it happened occasionally) was that they all had *huge* noggins. The theory still had some holes; did big heads cause success, or were they only a side-effect of it? Nunnally looked like a great bet; he had big hair, too. Big head and big hair on one individual was a dead lock, the equivalent of wagering on the one horse in a race where all the others are forced to wear plastic bags over their heads. I'd like to put a plastic bag over Nunnally's head, Barry thought.

Since his appearance as Valumart, through dinner and now standing in the reflected dumbosity of his scheme, Nunnally hardened, in Barry's mind, from the merely eccentric to the genuine article, an A-1, government-inspected, UL-laboratories tested nutbar. 'Speaking of New York, we have to—'

'Let's race again!' Ermine said, changing the subject. 'Trevor, I want to race you!' Their eyes unmistakably met, and Barry became pissed off as he saw their chances of leaving Planet Goofball tonight shrink to zero. It was clear that Ermine's libido – that great, impersonal force which created and destroyed at its whim – was going to carry the day.

'I guess we're sleeping here,' he mumbled to Lon, who paid no attention. He was on his hands and knees, engrossed.

'Vroom, vroom! Screech! CRASH!' said Lon, whamming Finland into Mozambique. 'Ahh! I'm on fire! I'm pinned under the car! I'm burning to death! Help! Ahh! AHHH!'

Disgusted, Barry decided to go find Dali and turn him upside-down. Maybe some money would fall out of his pockets.

Chapter Seven

IN THE BELLY
OF THE BEAST

◠◡◠

The next morning, Barry's first waking thought was (to borrow a phrase from the Jewish Wizards' Defense League) 'Never again.' Though Lon had the mind of a lil' shaver, as far as snoring was concerned, he was already in the full flower of manhood. Maturity might deepen his tone and improve his range, but he'd never be any louder than he was last night. So Barry was less than cheerful when Ermine bounced down to the dining room.

'Hello, guys! How was your night?' She was happier than anyone had a right to be before 10:30.

'Awful. And yours? Oh, forget it, I don't want to know.' Barry's empty stomach lurched when he remembered last night's final tableau: Nunnally, brandy snifter in hand, leading Ermine up to the Observatory to gaze at the square Moon that J.G. had put in. After that, his imagination mercifully went black. He couldn't wait to blow the whistle on this two-timer, once he found J.G.

'Awful? Why?'

'Because Baron Buzzsaw here sounds like there's a playing card stuck up his sinuses,' Barry said irritably.

'I said I was sorry, Barry,' Lon said petulantly, then went back to driving his pinewood racer over the tablecloth. As usual, sound effects were supplied, *con brio e saliva*.

'Well, that's too bad,' Ermine said, without real sympathy. 'Is there any juice or anything?'

'Why is your hair all wet?'

'Trevor and I have just come back from the loveliest swim in the ocean. It was like a warm bath!' She bit open a bobby pin, and stuck it in her curly mane. 'We saw a snake. It was scribbling figures in the sand.'

'An adder, I'll bet,' Barry said. He delighted in a rare opportunity to lord it over Ermine, factually, and poured it on. 'Deadly poisonous, filled to the eyes with neurotoxin. You're dead in five minutes, putrefying in seven. Was Nunnally bitten?' he asked hopefully.

'Very funny. Has Dali paid you yet?'

'No, he hasn't, thanks for asking.' The next time somebody asks you to buy a surplus airplane for a piece of conceptual art, say no, he reminded himself.

Ermine put a napkin on her lap. 'Well, after dinner

last night, he might give you a dead rat and call it even,' she said. 'Which reminds me, what outrage is slated for breakfast?'

Ermine was answered by a commotion in the doorway. 'Make way, make way!' Nunnally said, carrying a covered dish. Nobody was in his way, Barry thought. And take off that stupid hat.

Nunnally noticed Barry's glare. 'You like my tocque. Thank you. I thought it was appropriate after making this masterpiece' – he uncovered the dish with a flourish – 'toast with marmalade and pickles!

'The kitchen is full of auto parts and bubble wrap – we're having another banquet here tonight – so I had to scrounge around . . . What's everybody waiting for? Dig in!'

Quit saying that, Barry grumbled to himself. The flavors clashed so violently in Barry's mouth that he expected to hear cymbals. He swallowed it anyway. It tasted bad, but at least it wasn't more Art.

When they finished, Nunnally said, 'So! Off to New York, I suppose?'

'Yep,' said Barry. 'What's the best way? Is there an airport nearby? Or can we borrow Ms. Rollins' private jet?' he said, half-joking.

Nunnally chuckled. 'No jet here, but I'm sure you noticed our ocean outside? It's magically connected to the Caribbean, so you can pop over to the States quite easily. J.G. finds it *so* useful for business trips.'

Ermine piped up. 'So she takes a boat?'

'No, shark.'

The table exclaimed!

'Don't tell me you haven't heard of this. Shark travel is the rage among all the bright young things.' He smiled at Ermine, who responded with a smile. Barry felt another pang of nausea, so he jumped in.

'And how does one travel by shark, exactly?'

'They're very big, 75 feet at least – the smaller ones simply don't have the legroom. They open wide, and you walk right in. But their stomach has all the amenities of home, and has been hosed out, top to bottom. You can read, sleep, do whatever you like without fear of being digested. Then, when you've arrived, you give them a tickle and they vomit you up, easy as you please.'

Barry didn't like the sound of this, and his face showed it.

'Barry, I'm sure Trevor wouldn't suggest it if it wasn't perfectly safe,' Ermine said. 'He says his wi— companion takes it all the time.'

Exactly, thought Barry. In an effort to turn Ermine off the idea, he pulled out the heaviest artillery he could think of: 'It must smell like dead fish in there.'

Nunnally parried. 'Hardly. They clean it before and after every journey. Otherwise nobody would use it, even though it's frightfully fast. You'll be there in three hours.'

'Barry, come on, let's do it,' Ermine said. 'It'll be an adventure.'

Barry, drowning, grasped for the one remaining reed. 'Lon, what do you think?'

'Can I keep this car?' said Lon.

An hour later, after a shower, the three were down at the beach, staring at their conveyance with varying degrees of apprehension.

'Who'll be the first to board the S.S. Feeding Frenzy?' quipped Barry.

'Now, Barry, *corragio*.' Nunnally waded out to the immense shark. With every fiber of psychic energy, Barry sent a message to the fish: *eat him! Eat him NOW*! As usual, Barry was suffering a psychic brownout. Nunnally tapped the shark on the snout, and was suddenly standing next to an oval hole rimmed with green teeth. It was easily large enough to walk through, and, as Nunnally said, touching one, 'the teeth are all covered with kevlar mittens' – he pulled one off and waved it – 'so he couldn't hurt you even if he wanted to.'

'Put that one back on!'

'Come on, Barry. Don't tell me you're afraid.'
Nunnally was playing dirty pool. 'Children do it.'
Barry had a brainstorm: he grabbed the pinewood
derby car out of Lon's hands, and threw it into the
shark's open maw.

'*Hey!*' Lon yelled, aggrieved. 'Whatja do *that* for?'
He clambered in after it and climbed into the shark's
mouth. Barry and Ermine watched, waiting for the
nightmare to begin. Ermine thought to scold Barry for
the trick, but the truth was that she was as scared as he
was.

Lon's head emerged. 'Hey you guys! They got
Playstation in here!'

Good-byes were brief, but, in one instance, saliva-y.
Barry was glad as hell to be shot of the place and
especially of Nunnally. After sitting down, he pulled
out a soda from the mini bar.

'I wouldn't drink that,' Ermine said. 'I bet it's really
expensive.' Barry looked at her and cracked it open
with extra relish.

Ermine picked out a postcard from the rack leaning
against the gently undulating pink wall. The shark had
swallowed not only postcards, but recliners, a TV,
several varieties of snacks, a sleeping mask, Dram-
amine – really anything a traveller could want.

'Who are you writing?' Barry asked.

'Trevor,' Ermine replied. 'To thank him for every-thing.'

'What an idiot,' Barry said without venom – it was simply too obvious to be under dispute.

'Oh, you're too hard on him,' Ermine said, smiling. 'He's only idiot-esque. If you knew him like I do—'

Barry was set to make a pointed comment, but thought better of it. Their quarters – though easily the largest stomach Barry had ever been inside – were not expansive. Ermine, like many furry animals, looked cuddly but could be dangerous when cornered. Barry took a swig of his Morgana-Cola and belched. 'I can understand why you like him. He looks kind of like that guy from that group you liked. What were they called? 'N'Sane? 'N'Competent?'

'N'Grown,' Ermine said scornfully. 'I was hardly the only one who liked them. They had millions of fans. But since you do as well, I see your point.'

Barry was mildly affronted. 'At least I didn't have to resort to a Kuteness Konjuring.' He and Lon had a field day, after the Department of Magick discovered the group's illegal ploy. 'What a bunch of knobs, right Lon?' Barry said, laughing.

He laughed alone; Lon had drifted off to sleep. As usual, Lon's four limbs were twitching; during sleep, his dog-brain was in control. Barry heard the sound of swallowed barks. On Lon's chest there lay a small book. Barry carefully lifted it up, turned it over.

'Don't read that. It's Lon's. Maybe it's private,' Ermine said. Ermine and Lon had a 'thing' for each other, back before the accident, and she was protective. Barry ignored her, and read:

> 'Dear Dairy:
>
> Yu won't belev this but I am in a SHRK! A big big 1. I am siting in his stumic. It is cul and not as stiky as you think.Tuday, Ermn saw an adr (poysin sneke).Bary is bing meen as usl hee grabd my car and thru it. Wy is he so meen? It is *not rite* to tret frends that way.'

Barry replaced the book. Lon looked cute as he slept, in a sort of unsettling stunted man-child way. The fact that Lon was snoozing without nasal fanfare momentarily irritated him, he could hardly afford blows to his credibility, especially with Ermine. But this annoyance was more than offset by the fact that Barry could now sleep himself. Which he did – after taking an aspirin for his aching interrobang, and making a mental note to quit being 'so meen' to Lon. He shouldn't punish Lon just because he missed the friend he used to have before the accident. It wasn't Lon's fault he was a moron dog-boy.

A few hours later, Barry felt a pain between his third and fourth rib, where Ermine was jabbing him with her chewed biro.

'Wake up. We're almost there.'

Barry yawned and stretched. He shook Lon gently. In addition to having that scar-ache – *still* – he had the kind of brain-fog that comes from catching up on night-sleep during the day.

But even if Barry had been really awake, he couldn't have guessed why his scar had been paining him so persistently: attached to the shark, not six inches of undulating fishflesh away from his resting head, a remora loyal to Lord Valumart was attached, and taking notes. They could expect a warm reception in New York.

Besides being useful, the ability of Muddles to ignore magic was a running joke in the wizarding world. It formed the foundation of a rich vein of ethnic humor, for example: 'How many Muddles does it take to see a flying carpet?' 'That was no carpet, that was a weather balloon!' Okay, not so funny – but relations between the two groups weren't very acrimonious, either. The efforts of bleeding hearts like Ermine to stamp out such jokes (one of many Hogwash crusades) had proved mostly successful, but complete eradication was impossible.

However, as willfully ignorant of the magical as Muddles are wont to be, a 75-foot Iberian-registered *Carcaradon Meglodon* vomiting three smiling Brits onto the dock would be enough to make the most jaded New Yorker drop a dime to the nearest tabloid. So, the shark had to be sly. He swam over to the West Side, up the Hudson, to the Christopher Street piers, where the only onlookers would be transvestite prostitutes who would chalk it up to bad batch of blender drinks.

At the appropriate pier, with the various denizens of the sexual underground looking on, the shark hefted itself out of the water and threw up our heroes, who were gently propelled onto the weathered wood. After all three had 'disemsharked,' the fish smiled, dropped back into the water, and swam away.

'Do you have any idea where we are?' Barry said.

'No,' Ermine replied.

'Hey, mister – want me to jingle your bells?' an extremely bulky, hirsute lady said to Lon, giving his hat a playful pull.

Ermine grabbed Lon's arm. 'Let's go, Lon.'

'Hey Erm, hand me your cell phone,' Barry said. 'I'm going to call Ferd and Jorge.'

Ferd and Jorge Measly were several years ahead of

Barry, Ermine and Lon, their littlest brother. They had been full of mischief at Hogwash, and the school frankly hadn't been the same since their hasty, unwilling departure. They had been expelled – with only one semester to go – after Bumblemore had eaten one of their trick candies and grown an extra (nonfunctioning, thank God) penis. Everyone agreed that it had been worth it. Up until that point, the brothers' great claim to fame was 'inventing' crop circles, something even Muddles had noticed.

The pair had moved to New York, where they felt their anarchic genius would be appreciated. It was – one worked for the FDA, putting charms and curses on cigarettes to ward off underaged smokers, while the other demolished buildings magically for the City.

Unlike wizard pipes, wizard cell phones were no better than the Muddle kind; you often had to be a pretzeltongue to decipher what somebody was saying. Hearing (intermittently) that Barry and company were in town, Ferd and Jorge immediately spat out an itinerary of mayhem lasting several days. Barry got their address and hung up. The three hailed a cab, and Barry gave the address.

'How are we going to pay for this?' Ermine

whispered. 'I didn't get a chance to hex a cash machine!'

The cabbie recognized them immediately. 'You're – you're dat guy! What'cher name? Harry something?'

As if! What a stupid name! 'Barry, actually,' Barry said. They got the cab ride in exchange for some autographs written with Ermine's lipstick.

'Barry! Erm! Lon!' Ferd and Jorge greeted the travellers exuberantly. 'Come on in!'

Barry found himself in the dirtiest apartment that the inviolate dicta of Time and Space would allow. His screaming nostrils quivered in an effort to block out whatever was wafting from the fridge – it smelled like one of Ferd's Chinese-food-turned-science-experiments. Still, they were among friends, and that was quite a step up from Nunnally, Barry thought.

Other than the mess, the primary feature of their apartment was the bathtub in the kitchen – and the walls, which had been painted a Pepto-Bismol pink by a previous tenant. Ermine remarked that it looked like the belly of a shark.

'Huh? Whatever. Anyway, great to see you,' said Ferd. 'Want a beer? Lon, let me put some soda in a dish for you.'

'Let's go out on the fire escape,' Jorge said. 'It smells

better out there.' At least they smelled it too, Barry thought.

With much laughter and some spillage on the mangy shih-tzu yapping at them from the garden below, the five old friends caught up.

'How's your mum and dad?' Ermine asked.

'Same as always,' Ferd said. 'Loving and normal on the outside, perverted and dysfunctional on the inside.'

'Isn't everybody?' Jorge said.

'This is a cool old building,' Barry said. 'It's a shame they've let it slide.'

'We do our part,' Ferd said, saluting the group with his beer before taking a swig.

'What's this building called again?' Ermine said. 'It's rather famous, isn't it?'

'The Oneida,' Jorge said. 'Yeah, a lot of old-time celebrities used to live here. Before it got chopped up into littler apartments. James Dean, Carmen Miranda. A lot of actors. John Wilkes Booth.'

'It's haunted,' Ferd said matter-of-factly. 'I've seen the ghost.'

'You have?!' Lon said, excitedly.

'Sure, several times,' continued Ferd. 'He's an improv ghost.'

'What do you mean?' Ermine said.

'The story is that he was a poor improvisational

actor who died onstage one night. So he's condemned
to do improv for all eternity,' Ermine sighed over the
romance of it all. Ferd continued: 'So here's what
happens: you'll be walking down the hall, or closing
the front door behind you, and suddenly Tony – that's
his name – will be standing next to you, and he'll say,
"Is this the first time you've been to the doctor?" or
"Welcome to the Army, Private!" or whatever, and
you'll be forced to go through the entire scene with
him.'

'If you don't, he'll play tricks on you,' Jorge said.
'Like make your shower go cold suddenly, or make
your key stick in the door.'

'This building sounds like a super's nightmare,'
Ermine said.

'It is, and so are we,' Ferd said, smiling. 'So why're
you guys here?'

When Barry told them their ultimate goal, Jorge
frowned. 'That's gonna be tough. You're going to have
to kidnap her. Think about it: why would J.G. want to
stop the movie? She'll make a pile more loot just from
the merchandising.'

'I don't know, but we'll figure something out.'

Ermine chimed in. 'She's always struck me as a
reasonable woman. If we could only find out where she
is. Do you have any ideas?'

Ferd said, 'The *New York Ghost* said she was in St. Bart's with Ben Afflict and Courtney Lust last month, but that's all I and ten million other New Yorkers can tell you.'

Barry had a brainstorm. 'Hey! I bet Serious would know.' Serious was a schoolchum of his dad's and Barry's godfather, although the only religious instruction that Serious had ever imparted, was how to count cards in blackjack.

Barry climbed through the window and picked up the phone. There was no dialtone. 'Guys, you have jobs. You really ought to pay your phone bill.'

Ferd walked over, and tapped it with his wand. Barry put it to his ear, and heard a dialtone.

'We get it free that way,' Ferd said. Barry nodded, marveling at their irrepressible semi-criminal impulses.

Barry opened his address book, and dialed the last number his godfather Serious had given him. On the eighth ring, a gruff male voice picked up.

What was that accent, Russo-Haitian? Haito-Russian? 'Hi, may I speak to Serious Blech?'

'Nah, he's not here no more.'

'Oh. Do you know where he is?'

'No, but I remember t'rowing the bastad out. He had a whatchacallit, a hippogriff. Tore up the floors, crapped all over da place.'

Barry rolled his eyes. What was it about wizards that made them such deadbeats? 'Okay, thanks.' He then tried wizard information, dialing the number he had crank-called so many times, 970-WIZZ. He then had a very American moment: instead of hearing that familiar slightly harried Welsh-accented voice asking, 'What listing?', he was greeted by something very strange.

'Hi there,' a sultry voice said. 'Welcome to 970-WIZZ, where beautiful women with very full bladders want to fulfill your wettest, wildest fantasies . . .'

Barry hung up.

Chapter Eight

FOR SOME REASON, DOGS FIGURE PROMINENTLY IN THIS STORY

❧

Frustrated and a little nauseous, Barry put down the phone. He stuck his head out of the window. 'Serious isn't listed,' he said.

'Have you checked the Bowery?' Ferd joked.

'Hey, that's my untrustworthy, utterly shiftless godfather you're talking about,' Barry said, climbing out on to the fire escape. 'So you guys have *no* idea how we can find J.G. Rollins?'

Jorge shrugged. 'Haven't a clue,' Ferd added.

'Come on, guys! You two are – well, maybe not *major* characters in the books, but still – I find it hard to believe that you wouldn't run across her. That she wouldn't look you guys up occasionally, just to pump you for—' Barry quoted their favorite review – '"rich details to make the wholesome characters throb with a magical life all their own."'

'Nobody who's lived with you sods could call you "wholesome,"' said Jorge. '*Arse*-wholesome, perhaps.'

'Actually,' said Ferd. 'I know who might know how to find her.'

'Spit it out, you colossal berk,' said Barry, irked.

'You shouldn't say bad words,' said Lon quietly.

'There's a girl here who's, like, the biggest Barry Trotter fan ever. She runs the fan club for all of America,' Ferd said. 'She invited us to a convention, back when we first got into town.' He turned to Jorge. 'Do you remember that girl you met?'

'The bloody stalker, you mean?'

'You shouldn't say, "bloody,"' Lon said in quiet indignation.

Barry grew exasperated. 'Look, we'd all like to hear about your romantic misadventures, but please: tell me the name of this girl!'

'Barry, she's trouble—'

'I don't care! I just want to know *where the fucking author is*!'

Like a stick of old sweaty dynamite, Lon exploded without warning. 'Stop saying that! Stop saying bad words, Barry! That is bad and you shouldn't do it and I'm going to tell!' He then collapsed into outraged tears. Ermine comforted him. 'It's okay, Lon, Barry

~ 113 ~

will stop.' She gave Barry a dirty look. In his sorrow, Lon slyly humped her leg.

'Yeah, I will. Sorry, Lon.' Lon looked mollified, and the tears eventually petered out.

'Her name is Phyllis DeVillers,' said Ferd. 'I don't have a number, but I do have a website address.' He wrote something on a piece of paper. 'It used to be barrytrotter.com, but Wagner Brothers threatened to sue her.'

Barry read: www.BuryTrotter.com. 'I resent that,' he said, smiling.

They all climbed back into the dark little apartment. 'Barry, Ermine was telling me about her new boy-friend,' Ferd said.

'He's not my boyfriend,' Ermine said. 'I was trying to wheedle information from him.'

'It's the Mata Hari method: wheedle via the peedle,' Barry snorted. 'Has she told you about his plans to change the world?'

'Yeah,' Jorge said, chuckling. 'It couldn't make things any worse.'

'What about splinters?' Ferd chimed in. 'Erm, just make sure you don't say the wrong thing to J.G. when you meet her. You don't want to start a catfight with a billionairess.'

'I don't see that there was anything wrong with it.' Ermine said defensively. The others hooted with derision. 'I can't see who it hurt.'

It was consistently amazing to Barry how flexible people's morality could be when they *really* wanted to do something. They knew it was wrong, but made up a reason excusing it. He was glad he was made of sterner stuff.

'Hey, who wants to watch our illegal cable?' Jorge asked.

'Cool,' said Barry.

As they watched TV, they all drank cans of delicious, refreshing RhuTastic.[7] With the magic of like calling to like, the Measly twins had an incredible ability to find a steady stream of true-life mayhem, from shakycam police footage, to videoed pranks, to sadistic Japanese gameshows. Right now, they were watching a new reality TV show called, 'Geronimo!', where a bunch of volunteers are thrown off a small cliff. Whoever survives is thrown off again, until there's only one person left, the winner. Then the winner is thrown off, so the network doesn't have to pay and the prize rolls over to the next week. It was

[7] A promotional consideration has been provided to the author by the makers of RhuTastic, America's only rhubarb-flavored soft drink.

~ 115 ~

currently $428 million. Six months into it, people were still applying.

'I love the look on the winner's face when he realizes they're gonna throw him off, too,' Ferd said.

'BOR-RING!' Lon said. 'Turn to cartoons.' He was ignored.

'Oof!' said Barry as the contestant hit the ground. 'Look, he's still moving.'

'Jorge,' Lon said. 'What's this?' He was holding the lollipop he stole off Zed Grimfood's worktable.

Jorge took it, smiling. 'Where'd you get this? It's from our secret candy stash. By the statue of the one-eyed wizard.'

'I'll show you a one-eyed wizard,' Ferd mumbled, eyes still on the set. Barry chuckled; for him, potty humor was one of Life's most reliable sources of pleasure. (As you doubtless have noticed.)

'Shhh! Lon's here!' Ermine said. The brothers shrugged.

'It's not a secret stash anymore,' Barry said. 'A third-year found it.'

Jorge and Ferd laughed. 'Oh, God, I'm glad I'm not Nurse Pommefritte!'[8] A school full of students swel-

---

[8] Nurse Puppy Pommefritte drank, heavily, and it was rumored that a Grittyfloor named Penelope Browser went into the infirmary with a stomach ache and came out with a cat's gut. Now all she can

ling and shrinking, sprouting feathers, going mirror-colored. 'What was in there? Besides Flood o Drools?' Ferd asked.

'Diarrhea Creams, Blink Blockers, Spastic Rolls, Dandruff Babies, tons more,' Ferd said. It was unnerving to see how much pleasure such stuff gave them.

'But what's this one?' Lon asked. 'Can I have it?'

'It's an Ono's Fire-Breathing Lollipop, with pure napalm center,' he said. 'Japanese pain candy. You have to callous up your tongue or else it burns like hell. Acquired taste, Lon. I wouldn't eat it, if I were you.'

Barry put down Ferd's copy of *The Muddle World on Five Spells a Day*; all this talk of candy made him hungry. He noticed a bakery box on the kitchen counter. 'What's in that?' he asked.

'Cannoli,' Jorge said. 'Some girl in my office had a birthday Friday and didn't want them. I, on the other hand, do not care how big my thighs get,' he said, slapping an ample haunch. 'Have some.'

Barry got up and brought the box over. Picking one up, it slipped from his grasp. 'Oops,' he said quietly. How many of History's most fateful moments have

eat is milk and dead mice. Her parents are considering a lawsuit. Still, that Nurse Pommefritte is a *genius* with animal parts.

been announced by that homely syllable! This was no exception.

The carpet upon which it landed – face-down, naturally – was so foul, with crumbs and bitten fingernails and dry boogers worked so deeply into the weave, that it was impossible to figure out where the fabric ended and the disgusting matter began. The cannoli was worse than inedible now; it was contagious. Barry threw it away with a shudder. What he didn't realize was that this cannoli had been planted by the minions of Lord Valumart (one of whom worked at an Italian bakery) with a tracking device smuggled inside the cheese filling. If Barry had eaten it, Dork forces would've been able to plot his every move, until excretion or death, and they were rooting for the latter. Unbeknownst to our heroes, a day later a garbage scow heading to the Fresh Kills landfill in Staten Island blew up spectacularly. Why Barry Trotter was hanging out on a garbage scow, Valumart's underlings couldn't say. All they knew is that 'even the great Barry Trotter couldn't have survived that explosion, your Dorkness.'

Evil masterminds have been saying this for years: it is *impossible* to get good help.

'Crikey, look at the time,' Jorge said. 'We gotta get over to Astral Park.' Astral Park was a dimension of

Central Park visible only to wizards. This kept the crowds down, especially on weekends.

'Jorge and I play in a Parks and Rec Quiddit League.' Ferd said. 'Would you guys like to come?'

Quiddit, as everybody knows, is a game where wizards and witches fly around on mops trying to put a ball through a hoop. The hoop is guarded by a goalkeeper. In addition to goalies, there are Bashers, whose job it is to hit things: Brainers (the very type of ball that took a core sample of Lon's bean), other players, and in particularly slow matches, themselves. When Bashers would hit people, their victims would invariably yell, 'Quit it!' – hence, the game's name. It's pointless, and very violent.

Finally, there are the Sic'ers, who chase a flying, sentient meat patty called a Sneetch. Whoever catches the Sneetch gets a zillion points and wins the match. This is a very stupid rule because it renders all other facets of the game meaningless; on the other hand, it is very useful from a literary standpoint, since it allows for a speedy, dramatic conclusion whenever the narration begins to drag. Barry was one of the best amateur Sic'ers ever. He loved this mindless, brutal, guts-freezingly dangerous sport.

Ermine, predictably, didn't. 'If you guys don't mind,

I'll take a miss,' said Ermine. 'Kate Spade has the cutest wands on sale.'

'Kate Spade!' Barry said, aggrieved. 'You said you were poor!'

'Priorities, Barry, priorities,' Ermine said.

'Lon? Barry? You'll come?'

'Sure,' Barry said. 'It'd be good to mount the old mop.'

'Okay!' Ferd said. 'Here, put this on.' It was a purple robe which read, 'Ty's Bar' in white, Olde English-style decals.

After they had all changed into their Quiddit robes – which had an athletic supporter skillfully woven into the crotch, the easier to straddle those splintery mophandles – they trooped out of the apartment and into the street, their mops slung over their shoulders. Lon tagged along, but having him zooming around would've been asking for trouble.

'Guys,' Barry said, pointing at the mops. 'Won't Muddles freak out?'

'Nah, nobody cares,' said Jorge. 'It's New York.'

The new, 'non-meen' Barry dutifully held Lon's hand as they crossed the street into the Park. Once inside, they walked by the Reservoir. 'A kraken lives up there,' Jorge said, pointing towards the lake-sized tank. 'He's a bad mamma-jamma.'

Ferd laughed. 'Every so often, he plucks a jogger off the path and eats 'em, in broad daylight. Doesn't matter how many Muddles see it, the newspaper always calls it "a jogging accident."'

Jorge said. 'They put the kraken in there because they had an infestation of merdemaids. The kraken ate them, but now the City's twice as screwed!'

Merdemaids, *blech*, Barry thought, shuddering.

They got to the field, which was freckled with people in robes stretching, unwrapping their sticks, and trash talking before the match: 'What are you, a janitor?' Quiddit trash talking was strictly for appearance's sake. A couple of other guys on the Ty's Bar team walked over.

'Hey, guys,' Jorge said. 'This is our friend Barry. Can he play?'

'Gee, Jorge, that's kinda cheat—'

'Lift up your fringe,' Ferd said to Barry. Barry showed off his interrobang.

'You're kiddin' me! Heck, yeah, he can play! Hi, Bar! I'm Spud and this is K-Dawg. Evan and Herr Doktor are over there stretching.'

Introductions were exchanged. 'Tell me, Barry, why're you hanging out with these losers?' K-Dawg asked.

Barry started to respond, then K-Dawg stopped

him. 'I'm just kidding,' she said. 'Listen, you're not really allowed to play with us, and if they find out who you are, they'll totally make us forfeit. So you're, uh, my cousin Pierre from France, okay?'

'Okay,' Barry said.

'No, Pierre, it's *"oui"*,' Spud said. Barry laughed. It would never work.

And by all measures it wouldn't have, had the team opposite them, Brooklyn's own Nosferatu Heating and Cooling, been anything less than mouth-breathing troglodytes. They were all products of New York City's notoriously shoddy (and shady) wizarding schools, fly-by-night graymarket places with names like AAAAA Charm School and Swami Patel's Presti- digitation Palace. According to Mr. Measly, a lot of them had ties to the Magi-Mob – which eventually led, like slime running down a drain, back to Lord Valumart. If you were rich, you could afford to send your kids to the few ritzy 'magical academies,' but for these the waiting list started at conception. Or before, if you believe in astrology and oracles.

Anyway, none of these dim bulbs discovered the ruse, even after Barry's obtuseness forced Ferd to blow his cover: 'Pierre! The sneetch! Over there, Pierre! . . . *Pierre! Pierre*, I'm talking to you, BARRY!'

'His name is Pierre Baris,' Jorge added nervously.

He needn't have worried, because the closest opponent, 'Ox,' had a thick finger jammed up his nose and was fully absorbed in what he was encountering there.

As unhealthy as they were brutal, Nosferatu Heating and Cooling all smoked cheap, noxious cigars as they played.[9] Their mops sagged to a preposterous degree as they ferried the economy-sized goons to and fro. The opposing Basher, Barry noticed, had jowls *on his jowls*. These were so pendulous, they snapped in the breeze like a flag whenever he put on speed. Quiddit is not very physically demanding, but from the start of the match the men and women of Nosferatu were sweating like morbidly-obese clydesdales chasing the last sugar cube on Earth.

Unfortunately, there was one member of the opposition who wasn't fooled by 'Pierre,' and that was Barry's rival Sic'er, a delightful gentleman nicknamed 'Meat.'

As Ty's Bar fell further and further behind (thanks to the rough play obligatory for opponents of Barry Trotter), it became clear that (as usual) Barry's team could win only if he caught the Sneetch. After Nosferatu muscled through another seven goals, Barry

[9] Wizard cigars have a dial on the side of them, which allows the smoker to set the level of smell emitted. Team Nosferatu had all theirs on full-blast.

realized this, and doubled his concentration. So did Meat, who zoomed over to him and growled, in a thick Brooklyn accent, 'I know who yeh are, ya wormwood. Yer not going anywhere.' As he said this, Meat clamped a simian-strong hand on the end of Barry's mop. Barry saw that pinned to his robe was a button with the same 'no Barry Trotters' symbol worn by the evil toboggan man back in Chapter 3 or 4, somewhere around there. Barry's scar danced a jig of discomfort.

'Let go, Meat!' Barry yelled. Meat laughed. Barry tried to accelerate away, but his mop – a cheap Slopsucker Seven – creeped forward, screeching and groaning with the effort of dragging Meat's added bulk. Wisps of foul black smoke began to appear; the mop was burning out.

Meat was delighted. 'When yer mop craps out, I'm lettin' go, and it's bye-bye Barry!'

'Barry, the Sneetch!' Jorge yelled, forgetting their trickery after too many bashes to the head. The Sneetch – not star-bellied like English ones, Barry noticed – glimmered forty feet below, near the ground. Barry swung his mop around and began to descend slowly; he hoped the Sneetch wouldn't look up from the magazine it was reading, see him, and zoom away. He hoped that his broom would make it. Meat yanked harder, even throwing his mop (a much more powerful

Puddleman 2000) into reverse. A great plume of acrid smoke was now pouring from Barry's mop, as it burned the last of its oil. Barry heard Meat coughing, then the ominous screech of metal against metal.

Ten feet from the ground, the smoke became too much for Meat and he let go. Barry leapt forward, and grabbed the startled, slightly greasy Sneetch. ('You crumpled my magazine!' said a tiny outraged voice.) At the same moment, his broom – which was only standard Parks and Rec issue, after all – gave out, and he tumbled to the ground. Luckily he didn't have far to fall, and the turf was soft – but his already sore ankle got a twist.

'*Yeouch*! Son of a witch, that hurts!' Barry yelled, and held up the Sneetch who was frying angrily against his palm. 'I got it!'

'We win!' Ferd yelled.

Ty's Bar reveled in their victory (not that it was such a shocker, given who this book is about). The men and women from Nosferatu were glad to have the game over, and departed immediately to attend to the afternoon's *real* work: drinking and getting into fights. When Barry caught the Sneetch and sealed Nosferatu's fate, they didn't even touch down – they just gave a few obscene gestures and zoomed off towards their pub. Barry alone knew how dangerous the 'friendly' game had been.

As the sweaty warriors of Ty's congratulated each other around a tub of sports drink (which Ferd had spiked), a mink-coated woman walked a poodle on the path below. A runty specimen even for that pint-sized breed, the rheumy-eyed dog somehow broke free, and ran over to the crowd, with its owner in leisurely pursuit. The escapee, feeling amorous, made a beeline for Barry, and began to vigorously hump his leg.

'You go, guy!' Lon said. 'Get some!'

'I'm so sorry,' a well-upholstered, homely matron said to Barry, as she pulled the dog off. She buckled a little as the scent of ten sweaty witches and wizards slammed into her olfactory organs. 'Come on, *mon petit.*' Coughing, she retreated to the path, pulling the yapping, straining, unwilling little pooch behind her.

'That dog looked so familiar,' Barry said to no one in particular. 'I swear I've seen it somewhere before.'

'I think Barry's fallen in love,' Spud said, and the others joined in.

'Ferd, Jorge, wait here,' Barry said. 'If I'm not back in 15 minutes, take Lon home.' Then he ran after the lady, who was heading out of Astral Park.

He followed her for the rest of their walk, keeping

well behind so that she couldn't see (or smell) him. As the pair entered a posh building on Astral Park West, Barry saw a surprisingly tough, seedy-looking door-man touch his cap and let them in.

Barry stopped at the edge of the Park, crouched in the bushes, and contemplated his next move. Before he could decide, the dog came sprinting out of the building, trailing its leash. Eluding the doorman, the dog dashed across the street, narrowly missing a squishy death several times.

The poodle was heading straight for him. 'Come on, boy, come on!' Barry yelled, crouching down with open arms to encourage the dog. The dog ran right past him, into the Park.

The red-haired matron (even from across the street Barry could see that it was a dye job), hollered, 'Hey, young man! Get my dog back, and I'll give you $1000! *And* a plaster cast of Art Valumord's todger!'

When somebody makes an offer like that, and you're as big a fan of VTA as Barry was, you don't stop to ask questions like, 'Where would I put it?'. Barry turned and ran into the park. He had gotten about 100 yards down the path and hadn't seen any sign of the poodle when he heard a hoarse voice.

'Hey, Barty! Over here,' A shabby-looking man in a worn old tuxedo about three sizes too small was crouching behind a bush. Looking around, he motioned Barry over.

It was none other than his godfather, Serious Blech.

Chapter Nine

THE PRISONER
OF AZTALAN

✺

Great to see you, Barty,' Serious wheezed, still recovering from his dash to freedom. He always got Barry's name slightly wrong. At first Barry thought he was trying to be funny; now he thought it was just another irritating facet of Serious' thoroughgoing insanity. 'You've finally conquered those spots.' Barry's face was still lightly pocked from Valumart's attack several years ago, which his fans knew as *Barry Trotter and the Acne of Fire*. Barry remembered the publicity tour for that book quite unfondly.

'Watch it, mate,' Barry said in (mostly) mock anger. 'Can you help me snag that plaster cast?'

Serious grew serious. 'Perish the thought, Beany. That's how I got into this predicament. Two years ago, I caught Mrs. Throttlebottom's dog and brought it back to her. I've been her excruciatingly-reluctant love slave ever since.'

'What? I don't understand.'

'Minerva Throttlebottom's loaded – her first husband made a tidy packet in wart remover. She was his test subject, and boy, did she earn every penny. Maybe you couldn't tell from where you were standing, but trust me. Nobody'd kiss her unless they were compelled to by powerful Dork magic.'

'Oh, I get it,' Barry said. 'You were doing the old "kept man" routine and got a little more than you bargained for.'

Serious looked around, making sure that Throttlebottom hadn't come after him. 'No, no – well, yes. But she tricked me. She said that she'd give me the secret formula to Coke.'

Barry whistled. 'She sure had your number.'

'Yours, too, I note,' Serious retorted. 'She uses an enchantment to find out what you covet most. She's a sort of Siren of goods and services. Once you're inside, you can't leave her apartment until you touch a relative. You were that relative – close enough for purposes of the curse, I guess,' Serious said. 'She killed her old dog, a school friend of your father's and mine named Cecil Squiffington, right in front of me. She threw him into a big vat of wart remover, and he just dissolved. It was sad. And all because Cyril collected Charles and Di memorabilia.'

'Wow,' said Barry.

'That whole building is full of Dork magicians. "Drovatull Arms" . . . "Lord Valumart's", get it?'

'That anagram thing again,' Barry said. 'How dim does he think we are?'

'Pretty dim,' said Serious, 'and he's usually right, Barney. Let's get out of here, just in case Minerva gets brave.'

He brushed the dust off and they started to walk, 'So, do you still like "Doctor Whom"?' Barry had sewn a Doctor Whom patch on his Army jacket last year, simply for irony's sake, and while most people Barry's age got the joke, Serious didn't. The first time Serious had met Barry, Barry was going through a Doctor Whom phase – wearing long, ugly scarves, mucking about in police boxes, perming his hair, the whole lot. While Barry hadn't seen the show in five years and hadn't liked it in seven, that was clearly still stuck in Serious' head. Barry equals Doctor Whom. Until death.

Barry supposed that it was simply misguided sentimentality that had saddled him with such a useless holepocket for a godfather. 'Me and your dad were best mates at Hogwash, Billy,' Serious told Barry for the umpteenth time. 'Held his head over the bowl after many a drunken revel. Emptying the contents of your stomach in the presence of another ... it may not have happened to you yet, but it'll happen someday, and I'm here to tell you: it's an unbreakable bond, son.'

Barry fought against the familiar feeling of way too much information. As they walked through the park, Serious scanned the ground for dropped change. He picked up a scuffed washer, then threw it away.

'Yes, Britney, I take my position as your godfather very seriously,' Serious said. ' I think of you as my own son, because that's the way your dad would've wanted it. There's nothing I wouldn't do for you. I want to help you along the road of life. Now—' he stopped walking for a second and faced Barry, placing his hand on Barry's shoulder manfully, '—can I borrow $50,000?'

Barry laughed in his face, amazed at his chutzpah. 'No way, Serious. Don't even try it. I've been burned by your schemes before.' He started to walk away – giving Serious money was like handing an arsonist your gas station credit card.

Serious followed. 'I know our earlier strategic alliances didn't turn out as planned, but this one is quite different. It's practically guaranteed. Anyway, give me a break. So the magic fuel pill was a fraud –

my engine got ruined, too! Nobody else got hurt; I was the one who the Errors hauled off to Aztalan.'

Barry shuddered at the mere mention of the place. Aztalan was the dreaded wizard prison, a Meso-American theme park lovingly guarded by members of a shadowy group known only as La Raza. Once you went in, it was said that they fed you tons of delicious, very greasy, jalapeño-filled food, but *nothing to drink*. When you begged for relief from the chili-fueled heat, they gave you Mexican water straight from the tap. Then, they made you ride the rides.

Chimichangas, nausea-inducing rides, stifling heat, and Montezuma's revenge meant that prisoners grew to loathe Aztalan more than any regular jail. Strong men melted away; hairy men grew bald; obnoxious men grew quiet. But nobody ever stayed the same, nor did they, in the end, survive. Serious had survived Aztalan – the only person ever – by following two rules: one, always sit in the front car, you get jostled less; and two, don't drink the water. 'No ice, no lettuce, nothing. I lived on that queer tamarind soda and sangria smuggled in by a bribed guard,' he confided to Barry.

After years of riding the Pinat-a-Whirl morning, noon, and night, Serious escaped by using a secret shrinking spell. One morning, when the guards led him up to the admissions sign, he was just a mite shorter than it demanded. The guards were amazed, but rules were rules, so they let him go.

Anyway, that was years ago, and Serious remained as deeply committed to fraud as ever. *That* was his magic.

'Serious, I can't believe that you really thought there was a little pill you could drop in your gas tank so your car could drive forever. That's the oldest urban legend there is.'

'*You* invested in it,' Serious said.

'Yeah, but I was 14!'

Serious shrugged. 'The fellow looked like a scientist to me. How was I to know he was a few parts short of a spectrometer? My current associates are men of the most sterling character and fine reputation. Trust me.'

'Uh-huh,' Barry said, already feeling his wallet growing lighter. 'Why don't you just rob a Muddle bank and use that?'

Serious put on an offended look. It was surprisingly authentic. 'The Code, Boney, the Code. There are certain things a wizard must never do, and "magically manipulating Muddles for personal gain" is the first and most important rule. It's for our own good.' Barry gave a puzzled look; Serious continued. 'Forget money – without the Code, we could enslave the billions of them with a single spell. Within 24 hours, every half-decent wizard and witch would have their own private army. Where would we be then, as fractious as we are? No, fleecing Muddles with magic is definitely not cricket.'

'But putting the bite on your godson is?'

Serious paid no attention. 'I know a gentleman who can provide us with an endless supply of coal oil and fly ash. Do you know what that is?'

'No,' Barry said without enthusiasm. Serious could provide enough for them both.

'The secret ingredient of Goo©, America's favorite toy!' Serious said excitedly, making a bright little noise with his tongue for the copyright symbol. 'Only they don't know it yet.'

'You're off your nut!' Barry said.

'Kids love goo! They *relate* to goo. Goo's *one of them*. Remember when you were a boy, and you'd find some goo on the street? You'd play with it for hours.'

'Speak for yourself.'

'You'd poke it with a stick, get some on the stick, fling it at your friends! Try to get the dog to eat it, dance around it, try to push your fellows into it. What I'm saying is we can harness that wonderful, innocent, goo-loving instinct that every child has, and make a real *packet* off it.'

As they exited the park, Serious started sticking his finger into every parking meter they passed. 'All right, maybe fifty grand is a little steep. Can you give me a lightning bridge loan of 75 cents?'

'Not if it's for Goo©,' Barry said.

'No, I just want a pretzel.'

As Barry ransacked his pockets, his wizard pipe tumbled out.

'I see you've taken up the vice of smoking, Bernie,' Serious said. 'I used to smoke a pipe, until I had a rather unsettling experience.'

'What happened?' Barry asked, pretty sure he didn't want to know.

'Well, as you know, I am chronically short on funds. As a consequence, I am always being lured down odd paths bargain-hunting. This predicament was, I'm afraid, fairly representative.

'I had just begun smoking a pipe, and was enjoying my cheap one quite a bit. I would smoke anything – tobacco, shredded newspaper, mashed potatoes, string – simply for the pleasure of it. One day, while passing my local tobacco shop, I spied a fine pipe for sale at an outlandishly small price. Someone had died, and they were selling off his – at least I think it was a he, it could've been a she – belongings right and left.

'I am not a squeamish man, so I purchased the pipe –

but it was only after I began using it that I realized why its price was so absurdly low. It was haunted by its previous owner. Quite aggressively and, I dare say, disgustingly.'

'Serious, would you be too offended if I said that, out of all the people I know, this would only happen to you?'

Serious kept talking. 'Hell's Own Meerschaum would light itself, go out at odd times, flare up most alarmingly (I lost more than one eyelash during our brief association) and the like. Worst of all, the mouthpiece would grow eerily cold and clammy, as if—'

Serious paused for emphasis. '—as if it were covered *in ghostly spit.*'

Barry snorted. He knew from experience that this story was almost certainly a lie, but that Serious would never admit it. If he admitted making this anecdote up from wholecloth, every facet of his life would be up for debate. And who knew how many 'facts' about him were out-and-out falsehoods? Serious did – and that's why he would never budge.

'It put me off smoking, I'll tell you that. Let it be a lesson to you, and a warning: never smoke the pipes of the dead. They won't stand for it.'

They had walked down to the bustling abdomen of

the city. When they found themselves in front of a particularly squalid construction site, a muddy hole waiting for a foundation, Serious turned to Barry and said, 'This is my stop.'

Barry was surprised. 'Boy, you're living rough, Serious.'

'Turn around, bend over, and look between your legs,' Serious said. Barry did, and saw a medium-sized building flying a big blue banner with two intertwined 'W's on it, 'The Wizards' and Witches Club,' Barry said.

'Pretty neat, huh? It moves around randomly to avoid prying Muddles – and property taxes. Wherever you see a big hole in Midtown, it's probably the Club.'

Barry was still confused. 'This place costs money, Serious. They'll throw you out on your ear.'

'The President is a friend. One of my investments made him a lot of money – something you declined, I might add. We have an understanding.'

'Fair enough, ' Barry said. 'I'm at Ferd and Jorge's apartment. Lon and Ermine are with me, too.'

'What's the reunion all about?'

'It's a long story, but the short version is: we're trying to stop this new Barry Trotter movie,' Barry said.

'I personally think that having a motion picture

made of your life would be delightful. If somebody made a movie about me, I could get money from Bill Gates. Still, you must have some good reason for wanting to stop it'

'Which I am not going to tell you, because if I did, it would be all over the Club in milliseconds.'

'You underestimate me, Beaujolais, really you do. But how are you all crammed in the boys' apartment? It can't be big,' Serious said.

'It isn't. And it smells.'

'I suspect that I could get you all some rooms here for a few nights. I'm sure they have spares,' Serious said. 'Think about it. It's the least I can do after you gave me back my freedom.'

'I will, Serious. Thanks,' Barry said, and the two parted. Despite his name, Serious was the least sensible adult Barry had ever met – or could imagine, really. He was pretty entertaining, if you avoided thinking about the collateral damage that habitually sprung up in his wake. Serious had no conception of consequences: for as long as Barry had known him, his godfather had been actually rooting for a nuclear war, because, in his words, 'The value of my comic book collection would then skyrocket.' Barry never had the heart to tell him what million-degree heat does to newsprint.

Chapter Ten

FANTASTIC!

I like this city, Barry thought, as he walked between the skyscrapers. I like the way it looks, how nobody cares if you're magical or not, I even like the way the bus exhaust Simonizes the insides of your lungs. There was so much action – music blared, electric signs blinked, crowds of people streamed in every direction, it made Barry feel alive.

It was past lunchtime, so Barry bought a hot dog. On a whim, Barry stopped at a pay phone, and called Fantastic Books; maybe they could help. The woman who answered said that J.G. wasn't there, and even if she were, 'we both know that Barry Trotter is just a fictional character.' Fantastic got about one hundred calls a day, an equal mix of pranksters and the institutionalized.

Finally Barry got tired of it and sent a charm through the phone line. Though spells are much weakened this way – please don't try this at home – she came around enough to connect him to Fantastic's public relations officer.

The flack, on the other hand, had no trouble whatever believing that Barry was who he said he was. *It was almost as if she had been expecting his call.*

She told him to come down to their offices, have a soda, and meet everybody. She seemed very friendly, almost eager to help; it was a nice change. Barry agreed, and called Ermine and Lon. Lon would like a children's book publisher and Barry was determined to root out 'meenness' in all of its forms. The trio were soon on their way to Fantastic's offices, which were only ten Quiddit fields or so away from the Measly boys' apartment, as the owl flies.

On the 39th floor of Fantastic Towers (called, with good reason, 'the house that Barry built'), Barry, Ermine and Lon all sat opposite a large desk in a nondescript corporate hutch. The name on the desk was 'Susan Thompson,' and she was Fantastic's Vice President for Public Relations. There was a window – Thompson was a comer, that's for sure – but the room wasn't large, and reeked of ozone, Windex, and strong perfume.

'So this is the young man who's made us so much

money. Welcome to Fantastic – can I get you all some coffee?'

'No, thanks,' Barry said.

The flack noticed Lon eyeing a stuffed animal on her desk. 'Do you like him?' she said. He nodded, and she tossed it to him. 'Keep it. That's our company mascot, Randy the Happy Rottweiler.'

While most men simply crumble, the hardness of the upper reaches of business has a tendency to hone a woman – particularly the ambitious and able kind – as sharp as a razor. All non-essentials of Thompson's personality had been sloughed off long ago. Whatever friendliness she showed was an annoying necessity, like wearing pantyhose.

Thompson told them about the company's illustrious history; it had started in 1903 as 'Kill-It,' a newsletter for teenage BB-gun enthusiasts, 'and currently sits astride the children's publishing field like a Colossus.' Sits astride? Ermine thought. She couldn't imagine being tucked in by her at night – she imagined recovering from that embrace bleeding slightly. And yet, the woman did have children, the proof was right there on her desk. They looked unhurt. Ermine guessed that she sheathed herself somehow before going home.

'. . . But enough of my chatter,' Thompson said,

flicking her glasses up on her nose. 'What can Fantastic do for you?'

Barry and Ermine both began to talk at once. For the sake of harmony, Barry let Ermine explain.

'Well, Mrs. Thompson, for a bunch of reasons, we are looking for J.G. Rollins. We need to speak to her immediately.'

'She's a very busy woman, Ms., uh—'

'Cringer.'

'Ms. Cringer. How could I forget, after reading all the books?' she lied, preferring an endless stream of forgettable lawyer-thrillers. 'Ms. Rollins needs peace and quiet to write, and while we'd like to help you three, our first obligation is to our star writer. Surely you understand.'

'But we have to *talk* to her. If we don't, Hogwash may—'

Don't tell her any more than she needs to know, Barry thought, and jumped in. 'Look, Mrs. Thompson. We need to talk to J.G.who I've met many times – who's a *friend* – and convince her to stop the Barry Trotter movie.' Oops, Barry thought.

Thompson was genuinely shocked, blanching at the possibility – then she laughed. 'Oh, Barry Trotter. I've read enough of your books to know that you're a trickster!'

'I'm serious. We all are,' Barry said. 'If I can't find J.G., I'm prepared to do whatever's necessary to stop it. I'll get arrested, check myself into rehab. Ermine here will seduce a politician . . . and Lon, well, he'll bite somebody. What I'm trying to say is, we'll stir up a shitstorm of publicity so unremittingly *awful* that the film will tank. And, you'll have to end the series.'

'End the series? God forbid. Why on Earth would we do that?' Thompson gave a hard smile. 'Barry, if you're half as intelligent as your fictional self, you know that you can't stop J.G. from writing the books. She has a right to practice her livelihood. And as long as there are books, there will be movies,' Thompson said. 'If the movie were a scatological, sex-obsessed parody or something, then maybe you could lead a boycott. But, as it is, the only person who can stop the Barry gravy train, in all of its many forms, is J.G. herself.

'And she's not about to, I assure you. There's much too much at stake.'

For a moment, Barry began to tell her what Nunnally had said. Ermine silenced him with a look; hold on to that trump card until the last possible moment.

'So I would suggest you relax, and enjoy all the attention.' The warmthless smile returned.

'Well, after so many books, I thought maybe J.G. was getting tired,' Ermine said.

'Not a bit – she loves to write Barry Trotter. It's what she was born to do. Yes, I think that Barry Trotter will only stop' – and now her voice grew hard – 'after they pry the pen from her *cold, dead hands.*' Ermine felt the plentiful brown hair on her arms raise.

There was a second of quiet, then the conversation returned to its original tapioca-like consistency. 'Would you like a tour of the building?'

'Sure!' said Lon, who was by this time very fidgety.

'All right, then.' The group trooped out of her office, and into the elevator. What followed was ten or so floors of typical corporate environment: beige carpets, cubicles, vaguely disgruntled employees, fluorescent lighting. There were only occasional touches – exposed ductwork painted primary colors, framed kids draw-ings – reminding you that the business was childrens' publishing, and not, say, PCs or tampons.

One exception to this blandness was the floor where they created magazines, filled with people keeping their constitutional anarchism under corporate wraps, for the sake of decent health insurance. In the space of five minutes, Barry, Lon, and Ermine were introduced to an experimental Jello sculptress, a musician who composed symphonies for fish, and no fewer than seven aspiring standups. When they passed through the art department, Lon saw another Randy on an employee's desk. Only this time, some wag had attached a big pink erection. 'That's my Happy the Randy Rottweiler,' the employee said subversively. Lon blushed and giggled. 'You're *bad*,' he said.

As they rode the elevator down to the lobby, Barry noticed a button that clearly read 'Torture Chamber.' 'What's that about?' he asked.

Thompson hesitated, then said, 'Oh, that's what our employees call the basement gym. We're a crazy, creative bunch here.'

Two faceless gentlemen in matching pinstriped suits got on. Barry was immediately seized with cold; it spread out from his chest, as if his heart had been turned to ice. The world began to spin, and he fell.

'I' Barry said, then collapsed.

'Oh my God, *Barry*! Lon, help me,' Ermine held Barry up.

'What's wrong?' Thompson said. Ermine thought she saw the shadow of a smile. The blankfaced men in suits looked impassively at Barry, who gave a small moan.

'We have to get him out of here!'

Just then, the doors opened, and Lon and Ermine carried Barry off the elevator. They lay him down on the carpet and Ermine pinched his face, which was bone-white. Thompson got off the car and the door closed. Barry immediately began to revive.

'I'm sorry,' Thompson said. 'I had no idea that he would be so sensitive to our Marketors.'

Ermine was apopletic. 'Those soulless bloodsuckers could've *killed* him!'

The flack tried to calm her down. 'I understand, Ms., uh . . .'

'Cringer!' Ermine barked.

'Cringer, but they are a regrettable necessity. Fantastic must market itself and its products, just like everybody else.' Lon growled at her.

'Ah, Barry's coming around,' she said.

Barry stirred back to life. 'What happened?'

'I'm afraid you met two members of our Marketing Department, Barry. I had no idea that you'd react so strongly to them.'

'I'm a brand name,' Barry murmured. 'They feed off my identity.'

'Well . . . I'm really very sorry, Barry. Look, we're having a small party tonight, celebrating the one billionth copy of Barry Trotter sold. We'd all be honored if you could come. It's at a club near here, Chez Spirochete.'

'Will J.G. be there?' Ermine asked.

Chapter Ten

'Oh no,' said Thompson, with an odd laugh that sounded a little like, 'I know where J.G. is.'

'We'll think about it,' Ermine said between gritted teeth. 'Right now, I'd like to get Barry some fresh air.'

Chapter Eleven

CHARLIE AND THE
MILDEW-INFESTED
USED BOOKSTORE

ᏻᏕ

The farther Barry got away from Fantastic's marketors, the better he felt.

'There's no way in hell I'm going to that party,'
Ermine said.

For once, Barry spoke with the voice of reason. 'I
vote that we grin and bear it and see if we can't find
something out. Did you hear her laugh? I'll bet she
knows where J.G. is.' Ermine admitted that Barry had
a point . . . but she didn't have to like it.

The three friends walked the busy cobblestone
streets of Greenwich Village. After wandering pleas-
antly but aimlessly for a half-hour or so, they found
themselves totally lost; uptown's orderly streets had
turned into a warren of winding lanes, each pictu-
resque but indistinguishable from the others to out-of-

town eyes. Ermine was on the verge of hailing a cab when they turned a corner and saw a shop.

'Tomorrow's Pulp Used Bookstore!' Barry said. 'I know this guy, I met him at a convention once; let's go in and say hi.'

'And ask him directions,' Ermine said. 'I'm sick of being lost.'

The door opened with a tinkle, and after two steps inside, the trio already felt cramped. Books were everywhere – in shelves that stretched to the ceiling, in musty scrawled-on boxes waiting to be sorted, in small kickable piles on the side of every aisle. Everything seemed to be in various comforting shades of brown; the buff of aged paper, the khaki of cardboard, the beige of spilled coffee, the ochre of cockroaches. A medium-sized man in a green cardigan said, 'Can I help you?' He had a slight English accent, sandy blond hair, and wore wire-rimmed glasses.

'Charlie, do you remember me? It's Barry Trotter,' Barry said.

Charlie immediately offered a hand. 'Of course I do, good to see you again,' he said, with a genuine smile. 'You were the saving grace of that entire convention. Ham-on-Rye, wasn't it?'

'Right,' Barry said. 'These are my friends, Ermine Cringer and Lonald Measly.'

Charlie shook their hands. 'I know their characters well – but we both know how true-to-life those usually are, don't we?' They all smiled. Charlie was himself the star of one of the most popular children's books in the world, but a case of incredibly severe adult-onset lactose intolerance made his next trip to a chocolate factory sure to be his last.[10]

'How's business?' Barry said. Lon wandered off to give the premises a good sniff.

'You can see for yourself,' Charlie said with a sigh. The store was empty. I make most of my money from a website. I sell videos – hard-to-find and children's, mostly – and movie memorabilia. My rent here is murder. I couldn't keep going if it were just books. People just don't buy 'em like they used to.'

'Speaking of movies,' Ermine said, turning to Barry. 'Can I tell him?'

'Sure, Charlie can be trusted,' Barry said.

'*Now* I'm interested,' Charlie said.

'We're trying to stop the Barry Trotter one.'

Charlie grabbed Barry's hand. 'Oh, I am *so* happy to hear that. I wish you all the luck in the world. I wish

[10] Charlie's author was one of the few who could give J.G. a run for her money, sales-wise; his classics included *BFD*, *The Tits*, and of course, the immortal anti-Oedipal screed, *James and the Giant Bitch*. He was dead, killed by a vigilante mob of school librarians.

somebody had stopped mine.' Charlie's tone became bitter – many days behind the counter were spent stewing about this very topic. He didn't talk to many people all day long, so when he got a chance, the words poured out of him. 'Willy Wunka was no hero! He was a meglomaniacal, high-handed, money-mad, crook!' Charlie's color rose. 'Do you know how much those boompa-doompas got paid? A nickel a day! My wife's a boompa-doompa. She hates Wunka like poison.'

'I don't want to be a jerk,' Barry said, 'but I always liked that movie.'

'Sure you did, everyone does. It's funny. But Gene Milder was the star, not the kid. Not Charlie. The whole thing was a total lie,' Charlie said. 'The real Willy Wunka was such a drunk he could hardly stir caramel and stand at the same time. And such a vicious bastard. Ask a boompa-doompa if you don't believe me.'

Charlie regained his composure a bit. 'I'm sorry that it was ever made. Mark my words, Barry: if you can't stop it, when this is all over, you'll feel the same way.

'So,' Charlie said, 'how can I help?'

'I don't know if you can,' Ermine said.

'Oh, I know!' Charlie said. 'Hold on a second while I dig around in the back room!'

Barry and Ermine browsed for a minute, then

Charlie came back holding a bulky light with a heavy metal cowl.

'This will stop them in their tracks. I was going to sell it on my website, but heck, it's for a good cause.'

'I don't understand,' Barry said.

'This is a klieg light, for use on a set. The first person who used it was Orson Welles. Then, it was passed down from director to director, moving from lot to lot, ruining careers,' Charlie said. 'It's cursed. No picture that uses it will ever get finished. Guaranteed.'

Barry and Ermine looked at it. 'The legend is that a young witch actress was promised a part in *Citizen Kane II: Rosebud's Revenge* if she'd sleep with the writer. She was naive enough to do it, but of course the writer couldn't come through, so she put a curse on this light. That's why Welles' sequel to *Kane* was never made,' Charlie said. Ermine was dubious, but said nothing. Charlie seemed harmless, and besides, they needed all the help they could get.

'Check it out. You're the magical people, you'd know better than I would. Since you're friends, I'll give it to you for—' Charlie then named a price that struck Barry as exorbitant and Ermine as outrageous.

'Charlie, I don't know—' Barry said.

Charlie cut him off. 'Look, what are you planning to

do instead? Sabotage the cameras? Kidnap the director? Trust me, those studios are wily. They'll find a
way around it. Directors are like hydras: kill one, and
ten Alan Smithees will take his place.'

'Well ...' Barry said, weakening. 'Okay. Erm, can
you put it on your card? I'll pay you back,' Barry said.

Ermine grudgingly offered her plastic. 'Oof, it's
heavy,' she said, holding the light with both hands.
'Can we pick it up when we need it?'

'Sure,' Charlie said. Ermine waved her wand over it.
Now it would transport itself from Charlie's storeroom
to wherever she was, upon command. Magic could be
damn useful.

'If I buy this, will you read it to me?' Lon, said,
showing Barry a copy of *A Good Night to Moon*.

'The book that bared a million bottoms,' Barry said,
reading the back. 'Ermine, would you ... ?'

'Hey, since when am I Ms. Moneybags?'

'I just thought, since I'm going to read the book, you
could pay for it.'

'All right,' she said, taking her card back out and
slapping it down. 'What *is* it about guys and dropping
trou?'

'It's genetic,' said Charlie.

'It's pathetic,' said Ermine.

It was a beautiful evening, the kind that comes once or twice a fall, when the best parts of both seasons are mixed to perfection, like the elements of a properly-cast spell. At dusk, after a bright blue day, it was still warm enough to walk in shirtsleeves (or light robes, if you prefer). A breeze dodged in occasionally. It was an evening where everyone you pass on the sidewalk is going out to dinner.

But Barry, Lon and Erm had weightier things to attend to. After a coffee at a sidewalk café – Barry needed a jolt; his ordeal with the marketors had been draining – they headed to Chez Spirochete.

When they arrived, Barry turned to Lon and said, 'Act old, okay?'

'Sorry – private party,' the bouncer said.

'Yeah, we know,' said Barry, flashing their invitations. They got their hands stamped and walked in.

The club had a vaguely medical motif; all the waitstaff was wearing surgical scrubs as they scooted to and fro, taking orders on clipboards. Ermine noticed that the bartenders (all cute) were all wearing hospital gowns, which revealed their bottoms. Drinks were served in beakers or drip bottles; bar food was served in bedpans.

They got a table, and Barry called Jorge and Ferd. He described the mark the bouncer gave them, confident that the brothers could reproduce it via magic – they had been doing that kind of thing for years. Within the hour, they were sitting beside him.

The party was dead; the bosses all stayed on one side, drinking mineral water and talking about stock options. The underlings, without hefty portfolios to buffer their troubles, attacked the open bar with a vengeance.

A steady stream of employees came over to fawn and grovel, but Barry felt awkward. Lon was content enough to drink his kiddie cocktails and make Jorge's spent limes talk to each other. Ermine was ogling the bartenders shamelessly, and, if gross motor skills were any sign, was feeling no pain. She 'accidentally' spilled a drink on Susan Thompson, who likewise pretended to act graciously. There was a whiff of cat in the air.

Barry tried to chat up some employees (the pretty, young ones, obviously), to find out where J.G. might be, but in the hour before intoxication descended like the mists of the Forsaken Forest, he got precisely nowhere.

Dejected and getting a headache from the cigarette smoke, he turned to Ferd and Jorge, who were playing a drinking game involving enchanted coasters. 'You guys wanna get out of here?'

'Sure,' said Ferd.

'That's all right,' said Jorge, 'I'll stay here and make sure Lon and Ermine get home okay.'

'Ermine might not want to get home,' Ferd said.

'Noted,' said Jorge.

After Barry got his army jacket from the coat check, he and Ferd stood on the street. It was drizzling.

'Man, that was worse than the Silverfish Ice Cream Social,' Barry said. 'If that's being an adult, leave me out.'

Ferd smiled. 'I had forgotten about those,' Ferd said. 'Being a grownup isn't so bad.'

'Yeah, but your apartment—'

'What about it?' As they walked to nowhere in particular, Barry began to cite the many weirdnesses of the Measly duo's living quarters, from the Pepto-pink walls to the singing bathtub in the kitchen and the crunchy carpet. Ferd let Barry speak for awhile, then said, 'Let's change the subject. What do you want to do?'

'Look at that,' Barry said. High in the night sky, two dragons – a Connecticut Blueblood and Newark Needletail – wheeled, sizing each other up. 'I bet it's a drug deal gone bad,' Ferd said. The pair watched, waiting for the mayhem to begin.

Quick as a flash, wizards from the Metropolitan Magic Authority whizzed in between them to break up the fight. Back in World War Two, a dragon slammed into the Empire State Building as part of a frat prank. The MMA had to cast spells for years so that the Muddles thought it was a bomber accident.

They stopped inside a wizard bodega and Ferd got a packet of beenuts. They buzzed in your mouth.

'I can't believe you eat those,' Barry said. 'They jiggle your fillings.' Ferd shrugged. A few blocks later, they passed a large sign that read, 'Genital Readings, $5.'

Barry was just drunk enough to consider it. 'Let's do it, Ferd. Let's get a reading.'

'Nahhh,' said Ferd. 'I don't want some old weirdo prodding my weewee. I got enough of that from Alpo.'

Barry laughed. 'Come on, maybe she can tell us where J.G. Rollins is.' He tugged at Ferd's arm.

The alcohol quietly dissolved Ferd's better judgment – not that there was much of it to began with – so they walked in. They were greeted by several generations of heavily-mustachioed females, doubtless all genito-mancers; the skill was rumored to be genetic, unteachable. The oldest paid no attention to their arrival, sitting in a high-backed chair by a window watching the traffic, rooting for a collision. The youngest was similarly transfixed by a large television, which blared a shoddy, insipid cartoon. Illustrations covered the walls of the dimly-lit room, each one slightly mystical but so explicit Barry was embarrassed to even look at them.

Every piece of furniture was covered with plastic. Barry seemed to remember hearing in Madame Tralala's class that having a lot of plastic slipcovers around helped seeing the future. Or he could have been misremembering. Barry could 'remember' any fact, no matter how outlandish. Did he hear that or didn't he? Did he learn a fact, or make it up? Back and forth he went; it was like having hiccups of the brain.

The third woman – who could've been anywhere between 25 and 60 – looked up from a book and greeted them. 'Welcome boys. I am Madame Charlemagne. Are you here for a quick glance, or the full reading?'

'Uh, quick'

'*Full* reading,' Barry said.

'All right. I will take one of you at a time.' She snapped on a pair of latex gloves. 'Come with me. Step inside the beaded curtain and unbuckle.'

For reasons of decorum, we will leave the details of the readings to the mists of Time. Suffice to say that Madame Charlemagne was no fraud; and that Ferd and Barry each learned something of great importance.

Ferd learned that his path in life would have many twists and turns, though not so many that she would recommend plastic surgery. And what Barry learned made him grab Ferd and sprint back to the club as fast as he could.

They pushed to the front of the line, showed the bouncer their stamped hands, and ran through the gloomy club, spilling people's drinks, looking for Ermine. The blacklight that bathed every room made it nearly impossible to find anyone. They searched in vain – but then, Ferd spotted a flash of brassiere over in a corner.

'I found her, Barry!' he yelled over the music.

'She's up to her old tricks!' Barry yelled. Ermine, when she had too much to drink, became an exhibitionist. Her friends knew every freckle on her body. They were sick of it, frankly, but as Jorge said, 'At least she isn't a mean drunk.'

Barry and Ferd wended their way through the crowd. When they got to Ermine, she gave them both a big hug and kiss. She was blitzed.

'Put your sweater back on,' Barry hollered. 'We know where the author is!'

'Guys! I know where the author is!' Ermine yelled, not hearing a word.

'What?' Ferd and Barry yelled.

'What?' Ermine yelled.

Just then the song ended, breaking the impasse. 'I know where J.G. is,' Ermine said.

'How?' said Ferd. 'Did you get your fanny read?'

'What?' Ermine was completely befuddled. The deafening music started again, so they moved to a quieter hallway to sort it all out.

'So now we know she's at Fantastic,' Barry said. 'That's a start. Now the question is: Do we break her out ourselves, or wait for a wandering acromandela to do it for us?' As any reader of *Fabulous Beasts and How to Prepare Them* knows, acromandelas were gigantic black spiders with a passion for civil rights. Unfortunately, they were also native to South Africa, not Manhattan.

'We can't wait. I say we do it ourselves,' Barry said. They had rounded up Jorge and Lon, and repaired to Tiny's, a local subterranean jazz joint favored by New York's centaur community. Ferd and Jorge were fans of the club's regular 'charm slams,' where men with goatees and women with stringy hair tried out their latest free-verse incantations.

The entrance to Tiny's was a steam-release tube, in the middle of Seventh Avenue, in Greenwich Village. No matter how closely they looked, Muddles could only see the plastic orange tube, with steam pouring out of the top, a common sight in New York. Wizards and other magical creatures, however, could walk into the tube through a secret space in the side, down some steps, and into Tiny's.

A quartet ran through the final chords of 'Relapsin' at Camarillo,' then an emcee appeared onstage. 'Witches and Wizards, centaurs and centrinas, I give you ... Miss Spatula Clark!' He placed a wicker-bottomed Chianti bottle on the stage. Pink smoke began to pour from the spout, and formed the lumps and curves of a woman. The vaporous chanteuse began to sing. 'It's witchcraft ... cra-zy witchcraft ...' There was much applause. The ghost of Frank Sinatra wandered the club, slugging people – but, as a ghost, his fist passed through everyone harmlessly.

Jorge said, 'Are we sure J.G. even wants to leave? Do we tell her we're kidnapping her?'

'I don't think that will be necessary anymore. My guy told me she lives in the basement, in a teensy little cell,' Ermine said. 'The floor's electrified, and whenever she drops below a certain number of words per minute, she gets a shock. I think she'll be glad to get out of there, and grateful enough to help us.'

The males at the table were all transfixed by the smoky singer, who was constantly shifting shape into different women, all beautiful. Ermine felt the familiar irritation of being surrounded by cavemen. 'Stick with me, guys. We have a job to do. Any ideas? How can we get to her?'

Jorge said, 'Well, it's probably nothing, but there's going to be a Fantastic Board of Directors meeting tomorrow. Everybody at the party was talking about it.'

'That's good,' Ermine said. 'A lot of unfamiliar people coming and going's good.' Her wheels were turning. The band played and everybody thought. Phantom Frank stalked around, attempting to brawl.

'If I transformed myself into an overhead projector—' Barry offered.

'—everybody would be watching you. And besides, Barry, we all need to get in there, just in case things get sticky. I have a better idea,' Ermine said. Barry hated being cut off, but let her go on.

'Any big meeting like that, they always order in food. I'll pretend to be the caterer, and bring in a bunch of bagels.'

'I'm sure they'll appreciate your thoughtfulness,' said Barry.

Ermine rolled her eyes. 'You're the bagels! You and Lon and Ferd and Jorge. I'll transform you.'

'Good plan,' Jorge said. 'I've always wanted to tour the alimentary canal of a publishing fatcat.'

'Don't worry, Jorge, I'll put some real bagels on top. They'll eat those, and leave you to get stale.' Ermine said.

They all thought for a moment, except for Lon, who never did, and Ferd, who had fallen asleep. Barry broke the silence. 'I think it's a stupid idea,' – Ermine opened her mouth in protest – 'but since it's the only one we've got, okay.

'Let's get home and get some sleep,' Ermine said.

'You blew on some other guy's dice, babe! The Chairman don't stand for that!' Sinatra yelled at Ermine and hauled off. She didn't even notice; the haymaker passed through her chin without effect. *Dammit!* Sinatra hollered.

Chapter Twelve

THE GREAT ESCAPE

ᏩᎶ

While the rest of Hogwash's Finest were enthusiastically preparing to violate Fantastic's property rights, one alumnus was not looking forward to the running, jumping, possible bullet-evasion, and maybe even taser shots to the groin, that the morning held in store. Ferd had gone back to 'the 'Chete' after the rest of them had called it a night. He had rambunctiously greeted the dawn, with a nurse/waitress on each arm, and now he was paying for it.

He had quaffed some smart drinks – not a wise move for somebody of only middling mental capacity – and though the rush of abstract thought was pleasant while it lasted (he finally understood *Ulysses*, modern art and trig), the freefall back down to Ferd's normal IQ had produced the granddaddy of all hangovers. He had a big glass of water and read from the Encyclopedia Brittanica before catching a few hours of sleep, but it hadn't helped. Now, he alternated between weak moans and demands for his customary remedy, Jaffa cakes.

Gracefully suspended in the no-man's-land between biscuit and cake, these charming little orange-and-chocolate confections have no medical effect whatever. Nevertheless, Ferd had fastened onto them as his hangover palliative of choice, so six packages worth were now on their way from Kablooey.com.

The doorbell rang, and Barry answered it. There, helmet under arm, was the Kablooey.com delivery-man . . . and on his forehead was a perfectly-shaped interrobang.

Barry gawped. Did he have a long-lost brother? If so, could he get free stuff from Kablooey.com?

'It looks a shitload better than yours,' the delivery-man sneered. 'I'd be pissed if I had *that* shaky shit carved on my forehead.'

Barry exhaled silently. 'But . . . why?'

'I was totally into the books when I was a kid,' the guy said, handing over the crate of Jaffa cakes. 'Then I discovered girls. Sign here,' he said, handing Barry a clipboard. The deliveryman sighed, doing the wounded bird bit for a bigger tip. 'This is my last delivery; the company's going under as of noon.' Barry wondered if he was getting scammed, but gave him a fiver anyway. 'Thanks,' the guy said, and left.

Barry closed the door, and handed the box to Ferd, who tore it open with the ferocity of a wolverine. 'Thank you! God, my head is *killing* me,' Ferd said.

'Oh well, as Sartre said, "Life is pain."' Ferd didn't respond, chewing like mad.

'That was Buddha,' Ermine said.

'Same diff,' Barry shrugged.

'Let's blow this joint,' Jorge said. 'Since crime doesn't pay, I have to get to work by noon.'

Barry, Lon, Jorge and Ferd lined up and waited for their transformation into breakfast food. Jorge was the first to go, and he paid the price: he was turned into a bugle and a beagle before Ermine finally got it right.

'These wands warm up slowly in the morning,' Ermine said, shaking hers like a thermometer.

'Put seeds on me! Put seeds on me!' Lon yelled, hopping for emphasis. He loved poppy seeds. Ermine smiled; at times like these it was almost possible to think of Lon as a loveable little boy, rather than a demanding, freakishly-injured ex-crush woefully untutored in the ways of adult personal hygiene.

Once the boys were all bread, she put them into a paper bag, then walked down the street to get twenty more. She put them on top, much to the consternation of her cramped colleagues. Their muffled cursing soon stopped, however; Ermine assumed they were sleeping. She yawned sympathetically – it had been a late night.

She got into a taxi, and gave the driver Fantastic's address. Picking a moment when he was particularly engrossed in his cell phone, she waved her wand over herself and mumbled the ancient spell.

'*Cheesi-uni!*'

Ermine's normal togs were replaced by an appropriately horrible, sweat-trapping polyester uniform. A magical needle and thread embroidered 'Taste Sensations' on her matching green hat and overalls.

Ermine ran through everything mentally during the ride, so when she got to Fantastic, everything went smoothly. She got in the door; took the elevator up to ten; arranged the bagels quickly (and rather professionally, she thought) on the conference table; and was just about to take the bag containing the four bagelized humans back downstairs with her when a red-faced man in a boring grey suit touched her on the arm.

'Oh!' Ermine jumped.

'Why so nervous?' said the man. 'I won't bite.'

You'd do more than that, if you knew what I'm up to, Ermine thought.

'There's going to be more of us than usual,' he said. 'Better leave 'em all.'

'But . . . these are stale,' Ermine said, holding the bag close to her chest.

'That's okay,' the man said, taking it from her. 'We'll toast 'em.'

Ermine hoped her horror didn't show. '*T-toast* them?'

'Yeah, don't you do that in New York?' He dumped the contents of the bag on top of the arrangement. Ermine gulped. He handed her the empty bag.

'Hey, do you like Barry Trotter?' the man said, smiling.

'Doesn't everybody?' Ermine said, with just a hint of irony.

'I've got something for you,' he said, taking a bendable action figure out of his pocket. 'Who do you like better, Barry or Ermine?'

'Ermine? Who's Ermine?' Ermine said. 'I've never read the books.'

'She's Barry's girlfriend.'

'She is *not*!' Ermine said, forgetting herself.

'I thought you said you hadn't read the books,' the man said, laughing. 'It's okay, a lot of adults don't admit it at first. As long as you buy it, we don't care!

Chapter Twelve

Here, take an Ermine.' He held the figure's face next to hers. 'Wow, you two could be sisters!'

'Think so?' Ermine said, smiling weakly.

'We've just shipped twenty million of these to McDaniel's. I guess it'll encourage kids to scarf down more of that salty slop. Never touch it, myself. Bad for your ticker.' He picked up a pumpernickel bagel. 'Now, these are another story – low fat.' She had to fight an urge to knock the bagel from his hands. If she did, the jig would be up; but if she didn't, the boys would be eaten.

He took a big bite. Ermine expected to hear tiny screams, but thankfully, there were none.

'I'm Brent,' the man said, offering a crumby hand.

'Hi, Brent, I'm—' Ermine had forgotten to give herself a name. '—in a really big hurry, so if you'll excuse me . . .'

The only thing to do was to leave the boys to fend for themselves (as much as bagels can 'fend'), bust J.G. out as fast as she could, and come back for them later. Ermine excused herself, went to the elevator, and jabbed at the buttons ferociously. It finally came, and she pushed the button marked Torture Chamber. Gym, my glutes, Ermine thought. She descended slowly – the building looked new, but the guts of it were old. The

~ 170 ~

doors opened, and there stood a large security guard, his gun resting prominently on his hip.

'I'm sorry, Miss. You must have the wrong floor. This is a restricted area.'

Ermine played dumb. 'Oh, I'm so sorry.' How am I going to get past this fathead? she thought. 'Can you tell me how to get to the lobby?'

'No problem,' the guard said. 'Just hit "1", like so.'

The doors closed, and Ermine whipped out her wand, passing it over herself.

'*Anorexianervosa!*'

She was now the flack, Susan Thompson. It would be nice to get her into trouble, Ermine thought. When she got to the lobby, she hit 'TC' again, before anyone could enter. Their cries of protest died away.

The doors opened, and there was the guard again. This time, he stepped aside to let her pass. 'Good morning, Mrs. Thompson. The prisoner's been fairly quiet.'

Ermine turned. Trying to sound authoritative, she said, 'I've lost my key to the prisoner's cell. Could you come open it for me?'

The guard immediately smelled a rat, for he was smarter than he looked; Thompson *always* called the prisoner 'our golden Mother Goose.'

'You don't need a key, you just wave your ID in

front of the door. You know that.' He picked up the phone. 'Stay right there, whoever you are.'

'Oh, hell!' Ermine griped, and swiftly knocked him unconscious with a hex. 'I'll take this, thank you very much,' she said, unclipping his ID.

A moment later, she was standing in front of a thick metal door, with a sign that said. 'Nothing to See Here – Simply a Broom Closet – Authorized Personnel Only.' She swiped her magnetic card across the chest-high black plastic panel, and the massive door swung open. There, in the semi-darkness, was the once-proud figure of J.G. Rollins.

'Eeek!' she screamed, and cowered in the corner.

The room appeared to be made of burnished steel from floor to ceiling. Beside a naked bulb dangling harshly from a cord, the only implements in the room were a table with a typewriter on it, a prison-style commode, and a human-sized hamster water bottle. There was a shredded pile of *Publishers' Weakly* magazines in the corner, presumably where the world's most popular children's writer now slept.

'Oh, God, I just had the electrodes yesterday!' J.G. croaked. 'I gave you your chapter!'

How had it come to this, Fantastic holding its star author hostage? The fifth book, *Barry Trotter and the*

Order of the Penis, dealt with Barry's stormy puberty and fueled an ocean of inaccurately-erotic fanfic, as well as breaking all sales figures for the printed word. A risky choice, but one that worked. After the sixth book, *Barry Trotter and the Scary Magical Whatever*, critics accused her of becoming lazy. This was followed, however, by the ambitious 4700-page seventh book, *Barry Trotter and the Knights of Logorrhea*, wherein J.G. attempted to tie up every thread introduced in the earlier books. Lawsuits brought by readers injured by the massive tome necessitated book eight, *Barry Trotter Goes Crazy and Kills a Bunch of Lawyers* (which Fantastic made her retitle *Barry Trotter and the Briefcase Brigade*).

Clearly, J.G. was becoming unhinged, and stronger and stronger methods of coercion had become necessary simply to keep her writing at all. She cringed in front of Ermine, who waved her wand, and Susan Thompson was replaced by Taste Sensations Ermine.[11]

J.G. promptly stopped cowering, and stood up. 'I'm sorry, I didn't order any food,' she said. 'You probably got off on the wrong—'

'It's me, you nitwit,' Ermine said. 'Ermine Cringer.'

'Oh, thank God,' J.G. said. 'Please help me! I'll do

[11] Not available at your local toystore. Yet.

anything! I'll make you less geeky in the next book, I promise!'

'The first thing you can do is shut up,' Ermine said. The author looked a sight – she had come for a meeting with the Marketors, and instead had been hauled downstairs and pitched into this Krups-styled dungeon. For the last two weeks, she had lived a life of Dickensian servitude. Ermine surmised that she'd been wearing the same tasteful business attire for the entire time; the soles of her pantyhose had worn completely through, and the tatters flapped helplessly at her calves. 'Come on, ' she said, grabbing the fabulously-rich, dangerously undernourished writer by a slender arm. 'Let's get out of here.'

They ran – well, one ran, the other sort of staggered – over to the elevator. Both women jittered nervously as they waited. Several times the author started to speak, only to be shushed by Ermine, who was thinking hard. How could she get the author out? Have the boys been chewed up yet? And, should I buy those shoes I saw yesterday?

The elevator opened, and there – like Fantastic's totem spirit rising up in anger to protect its most valuable asset – was Randy the Happy Rottweiler.

Randy removed his head, revealing a balding young

man with bad skin. 'Sorry,' he said. 'Wrong floor. I can't see a thing through this head.'

Ermine and J.G. got into the elevator. J.G. was terrified, and she had a right to be, Ermine thought. She had no doubt that Fantastic would rather kill J.G. than see her go free and spill her guts to *Squawk*. The author couldn't prosecute them for her imprisonment – Amnesty International turns a blind eye to publishing companies – but she could hurt them in the place they'd feel it most: taking all that sweet Barry loot to a competitor. Suddenly, Ermine had a brainwave.

'What's a nice guy like you doing in a costume like that?' she asked.

'There's a school group coming for a tour at 10:00,' the man-dog said. 'They go bonkers for Randy.' He laughed bitterly. 'I keep asking, "I went to Yale Drama School for this?"'

'Great, that's all I wanted to know,' Ermine said. 20 minutes would be perfect. Pulling out her wand, she zapped him with a Soporiffic Suplex spell. He slumped to the floor of the elevator, fast asleep.

'Help me take off his costume,' she told J. G.. 'Start putting it on!'

By the time they reached the tenth floor conference room, the author was fastening Randy's head. They stepped out of the elevator, leaving the underwear-clad man slumped in the corner, dreaming happily.

'Follow me, and don't say anything,' Ermine said.

They walked to the conference room, from which the executives were fleeing, coughing and choking.

'There's something *very* wrong with those bagels!' one woman said, wiping her eyes. 'Those aren't baked goods, they're an obscenity!'

'I know, ma'am,' said Ermine, not missing a beat. 'I just got a page from Headquarters alerting me to a batch of bad bagels. I'll take them back, and make sure they're destroyed.'

'My God, I never smelled anything like that,' said another executive, holding a handkerchief over his nose. 'What's *wrong* with them?'

'They're highly experimental,' Ermine said. 'Made with olestra. Your H.R. people signed you up as test subjects.' She excused herself, leaving confusion in her wake. I wonder what happened, she thought.

Meanwhile, a group of execs were taunting Randy, poking him, slapping his snout. Ermine hoped that J.G. wouldn't rise to the bait. Keeping one eye on them, she hurriedly grabbed up the bagels and threw them into a bag.

'Hey, I'm eating those,' said a deep voice standing

behind her. She whirled around with a look of horror. 'No! I mean, don't – you can't—'

'Oh, I know, the smell. I shouldn't stand here and let it ruin my suit.' He took another bite. Ermine saw crumbs from his earlier victims nestling in a luxurious walrus moustache. Ermine listened hard for a tiny scream. 'But I lost most of my olfactory organs in 'Nam' (he pronounced this so it rhymed with 'jam') 'so it doesn't make any difference to me. I can't smell a thing.'

Ermine forced herself to look away from the jaws of death she was sure was remorselessly masticating one of her school chums. Well, nothing to be done about it now. She knew the risks of changing into a foodstuff, they all did. It was time to leave.

'Here, leave me a couple—' the man asked.

'No can do,' Ermine said, trying to sound briskly authoritative, like she thought an American might. 'Defective. Thanks. Bye.'

Grabbing the sackful of bagels, she strode over to the elevator and pushed the down button. It came, and they all piled in – Ermine, the executives, and Randy, who was still having a pretty hard time of it. Seasoned bullies all, the execs were enjoying a second spin through childhood.

'Come on,' one lout in a suit said, 'Let's see who's

under there.' He gave the head a tug. J.G. clamped her hands on his forearms, trying to remove them. They struggled.

Ermine jumped in. 'Uh, he's very sensitive.'

The lout turned to her. 'How the hell would you know?'

'He told me. He's got bad skin.'

The lout was preparing to invoke the f-word, when another exec clearly senior to him said, 'Bill, stop acting like an ass. We need to think about how to sell Barry to the Aborigines.'

She'd heard that voice before . . . on C-PAN's 'Kooknotes' . . . With a start, Ermine realized that she was standing next to the CEO of Fantastic Books. He looked harmless, like somebody's grandpa – which, no doubt, he was. Still, a bead of sweat trickled down her back.

Inside the suit, J.G. sneezed. 'Sorry,' she said, attempting a deep voice.

After descending several floors, the doors opened and there was Susan Thompson. Ermine faked a cough, trying to cover her face.

'All full up,' an exec said.

'I'll get the next one,' Susan said.

Just as the doors were starting to close, a hand shot

out and Ermine heard Brent holler out, 'Susan, look at this girl – isn't she the spitting image of Ermine?'

Thompson glanced up from the report she was glancing through, and looked at Ermine. Please don't recognize me, please don't—

'The real Ermine is chubbier,' Susan said. She returned to her papers, and the doors closed. Enraged, Ermine mumbled a few words, and ten pounds of unslimmable celluite appeared without a sound on Thompson's hips.

They finally reached the fifth floor, and all the executives piled out. When the door closed, Ermine allowed herself to exhale. She heard a muffled prayer of thanks issue from approximately Randy's neck.

They reached the ground floor, and walked towards the door. Would the security guard stop them? Had the sleeping actor or KO'ed guard been discovered yet?

The guard turned and looked. 'Hey Randy, the tour's waiting for you,' he said.

'Uh,' – change your voice, Ermine thought frantically – 'I gotta get something out of my car.'

'What, your flea collar?' the guard said, laughing dopily.

On the way out, they bumped into a woman in a uniform carrying a big bag full of food. 'Sorry,' said

Ermine, and realized that the *real* caterer had arrived. They'd better get gone, and quick!

As confusion erupted in the lobby, the two women hailed a taxi and gratefully sped away. Moments later, a man in boxer shorts ran into the guard, skidding to a stop on the freshly-waxed floor.

'Listen, man, you can't walk around like that.' the guard said. 'There's a tour group full of second graders —'

'That guy stole my costume! I paid a $250 deposit!' And the first few pieces of you-know-what hit the fan.

Chapter Thirteen

A BREAKING WINDFALL

ᏬᎱᏬᎦ

The untrammeled weirdness of Manhattan insures that the city's cabbies become tolerant to a fault. However, even in precincts as freewheeling as this, large terry-cloth mascots draw attention. The cabbie turned up his radio and hoped that these freaks wouldn't cause any trouble.

J.G. took off her head. 'Freedom!' she yelled, over the loud, reverberating cadences of non-Anglo music. 'I'm free!' She kissed Ermine impulsively.

The cabbie eyed them nervously via the rearview mirror. This was, after all, Greenwich Village.

'Just drive,' Ermine said. She didn't appreciate wandering eyes, not when she was getting ready to put the 'witch' back in Greenwich. Ermine picked out a bagel and put it on the seat next to her.

'Thanks, Ermine, but I've had enough bread and water to last a lifetime.'

Ermine tapped it with her wand. Nothing happened, so she tossed it out the window; it hit a woman waiting for a bus.

'What are you doing?' J.G. said.

'You'll see,' Ermine said, taking out another bagel.

This time, there was a split-second flash, and Jorge was suddenly sitting there, brushing sesame seeds out of his hair. Ermine transformed Barry, Lon, and finally Ferd – none of whom (not so surprisingly, given the title of this book) had so much as a toothmark on them. By the time she was finished, the backseat of the cab looked like a fraternity prank: Barry's foot was actually hanging out of the window.

'You'll have to pay extra!' the cabbie said, not missing a beat.

As they pulled onto Ferd and Jorge's street, Barry was the first to see the enormous crowd outside the Oneida, milling around malevolently. Somebody with a bullhorn was leading a chant: 'Please don't stop the movie! The movie will be groovy!' A few others were burning Barry in effigy.

'Drop us off here,' he said. 'Jorge, you've got Muddle money. Pay him.' Jorge slapped $10 into the driver's hand, and they all piled out, crouching behind the taxi door so as not to be seen. Somebody must have revealed that Barry was in town, and why. The whole thing smelled strongly of Bold Spice. Barry's interro-bang throbbed in silent agreement. They sneaked around the corner without being seen.

'We can't go back there,' Barry said.

'They didn't look so tough to me,' Ferd said. 'I bet they're all falsies.' Falsies were a zombie-like creature created and controlled by Marketors. They were usually found in packs called focus groups, ruining movies with their moronic preferences, giving stupid answers to poll questions, and electing idiotic politicians. Here's a rule of thumb: whenever you think, 'How could people be so stupid?' it's not people, it's falsies.

'Quiet, Gasbag,' Jorge said. 'Barry's right. Falsies and Marketors we could handle with a *Dontchu Believem* spell, but there might be Fantastic thugs in that crowd.' J.G. gulped.

'Let's go to Tiny's,' Jorge said. 'I bet they're still cleaning up after the overnight set. Mitch'll let us in.'

Minutes later, safely underground and amidst many bottles of Rhutastic and sandwiches brought from a nearby deli, the comrades celebrated their successful operation. Barry shook up his soda and squirted Ermine like it was champagne. High-spirited, slightly destructive – it was just like old times.

Meanwhile, the next shift of musicians milled

around in the candle-lit gloom, practicing, setting up, and telling jokes that apparently only other jazz musicians could understand. Neither group paid any attention to the other.

'So what happened up in the conference room?' Ermine asked. 'When I got up there, everybody looked like they were about to puke.'

The boys all turned to Ferd expectantly.

'I couldn't help it,' Ferd said, mumbling. 'I had really bad gas.' The old drinker's wisdom of

Smart drinks then beer, never fear

Beenuts, then smart drinks, nasty fart stink

had been proven vulgar-but-true yet again. Only this time, it had saved the boys' lives.

The executives had been hungry, and polished off the non-sentient bagels quickly. Luckily, the first one of our transmogrified heroes slated for a cream-cheese slath-ered demise had been Ferd, who had been brewing up horrific flatulence all morning (an unhappy by-product of the strange intellect-inducing concoctions he had tried the night before). Just as he was being lifted into the Vice President for Distribution's gaping maw, fear got the best of him and he let one rip. As usual, once one emission had been released, others followed, each riper and ruder than the last. Soon, the whole room was enveloped in a foul greenish haze, and Fantastic's braintrust had gone from coughing and dabbing their eyes, to unkind recriminations, to finally dropping to the floor and attempting to crawl for safety. Needless to say, nobody ate any bagels after that.

They were all laughing. Onstage a mummy trumpet player with a zombie rhythm section were warming up.

Thanks to rhubarb's status as Nature's truth serum, the conversation grew serious when Barry suddenly turned to J.G. and said, 'You're probably wondering why we busted you out. We need to stop the Barry Trotter movie, and we figured you knew how.'

At the mention of the word 'movie,' J.G. stiffened, and said in a loud monotone, 'I am overjoyed that Wagner Brothers will bring my creation to millions of new fans worldwide.'

The group was puzzled by the non sequitur. 'Uh . . . okay,' Ermine said. 'So, J.G., is there anybody at Fantastic that—'

J.G. spoke again, even louder this time. 'The people at Fantastic are the kindest, bravest, most wonderful people I have ever known.'

'But you can't be serious. Those Fantastic bastards—'

'The people at Fantastic are the kindest, bravest, most wonderful people I have ever known.'

'Wow,' Ferd said. 'I think she's gone bonkers.'

'I'm not so sure,' said Ermine. 'J.G.: movie.'

'I am overjoyed that Wagner Brothers will bring my creation to millions of new fans worldwide.'

'Fantastic.'

'The people at Fantastic are the kindest, bravest, most wonderful people I have ever known.'

'She's being controlled somehow,' Barry said. 'Hypnotized?'

'I don't think so,' Ermine said. 'J.G., stick out your tongue.' The author did so, and revealed a shiny microchip. Quick as a flash, Ermine picked it out. 'That's the problem. Whenever she hears certain words, she's being forced to respond in certain ways.'

J.G. looked groggy, as though she was waking up from a fitful dream.

'Thanks for taking that out. One gets awfully tired of saying the same things over and over.'

Jorge piped up. 'So that's why she's let Wagner be such bastards to Barry's fans all those years, shutting down websites, all that. Didn't seem in character.'

'It wasn't,' Ermine said.

'Lemme see that,' Barry said, and Ermine gave him the chip. On the back was engraved, 'Property of Z. Grimfood.' Barry was shocked – Zed was on the Fantastic payroll. Then again, it made perfect sense. Zed probably figured that helping the bad guys was the best way to get famous.

Ermine and the others explained the situation to the author, who looked progressively more aggrieved, and maybe a little scared, too.

'I don't know anything,' J.G. said. 'I've been in a cell for the last two weeks. I've got nothing to do with the movie. I'm sorry, I feel ungracious, but I don't have any power. I signed those papers years ago.'

Barry made a snap decision. 'Okay. If you promise to go home and stay quiet,' Barry said, 'then we won't have to kidnap you.'

J.G. looked offended. 'Am I a sack of potatoes to be lugged about and locked in the cellar by everybody?'

Ermine jumped in. 'J.G., of course we won't kidnap you. Do you know who's behind it? Who do we need to convince?'

'Oh, I know who's behind it all right,' J.G. said, and gave a queer, scared smile. 'It's Lord Valumart.' Onstage, the trumpet player dumped some spit from his horn.

Jorge said. 'Am I the only one who's not surprised?'

'*I'm* surprised,' Lon said. He was drawing in a pile of sugar with a swizzle stick.

'Look,' said J.G., 'If anybody knows how bright you guys are, it's me. And it's impressive how you've beaten Valumart so many times. But this time is different. Not only will you be going up against the

Dork Lord, you'll also be taking on Hollywood, and they don't mess around.'

'So what?' said Barry defiantly.

'They're a multi-billion dollar industry, that's what. Fantastic kidnapped me over a few million bucks – beenuts. You guys will cost Wagner Brothers a lot more: the millions they've already spent on publicity, plus the millions they're going to make for this movie, not to mention the next five. They'll play rough. There's no telling what they'll do. Remember, these are the same people who run the cable company.'

J.G. let this sink in for a moment. 'I don't intend on getting on their bad side. I've already gotten a taste of what they will do, and I don't have any magic to protect me.' She picked up Ermine's cell phone and began to dial.

Ferd realized what was about to happen, and slapped it to the floor.

'Chill, bro,' a musician said.

'Hey, that's my phone!' Ermine yelled. She picked it up, and pressed a few buttons to see if it still worked. It played 'Black Magic' when it rang.

'You're not ratting on us!' Ferd said. 'Move and I'll fumigate the joint!'

Barry looked serious, almost ... adult. 'Since you're useless to us, you're going to walk out of here, go back to Scotland, and pretend like nothing happened. You're not going to tell anyone, because if you do, I'll tell Fantastic that you're planning to quit writing the books.'

'That's a lie! Who told you that?' J.G. said.

'Your husband,' Barry said.

'Oh, *please*. Just my boyfriend. Trevor could never keep a secret,' J.G. said. Barry saw Ermine give a tiny start of alarm.

Barry continued. 'So take the first shark back to Scotland, and don't say a word until we've put a stop to the movie. If you so much as cough, I'll make a phone call to Fantastic, and you'll wake up with Randy the Happy Rottweiler sitting on your chest.'

There was a long silence. The author finally spoke.

'All right, I won't say anything,' J.G. said. 'Listen, they asked me if they could make movies out of my books. I did what any writer would; I said, "Yes, please!" And while I do stand to make a fair amount, I'm more interested in the possibility that if they make a movie, maybe more kids will read the books. What's wrong with wanting people to read my books?'

'And you don't care about what happens to Hog-wash,' Jorge said.

'She just cares about herself,' Ferd said.

'Of course I care about Hogwash. But that school was on its way out decades before I wrote a word. It's a dinosaur,' J.G. said. 'The best wizarding schools are all online now.

'Things change. Old-fashioned things are replaced. I love books – I spend my life writing them – but movies are what people want today. You can't stop progress,' J.G. said, then added with exasperation, 'I can understand you helping Bumblemore out for old times' sake, but why are you so angry at me?'

'Because you've made me into a fraud,' Barry said. 'Everybody thinks I'm this great wizard who can save the world with a wiggle of his wand. I can't – nobody can. I spend all my time either acting like the big, powerful jerk people expect me to be, or fighting with He Who Smells! Before you made us famous, Valu-mart just tried to make my life hard because he didn't like my parents. Now he's actually trying to *kill* me!'

'Plus,' Barry said. 'I never have any money.'

J.G. was quiet, cogitating. After a few moments, she pulled out a pen, and her checkbook, and wrote out a check. 'Barry,' she said, 'I can't make you un-famous, but I can help with the other thing.'

'Oh no, J.G., you can't buy me off—' Barry said.

She handed the check to Barry. It was for twenty-five million pounds.

'—or you *can* . . .' The check was so large, it seemed to vibrate in Barry's hand.

'That should be enough to take care of yourself and your friends. You could go someplace new, change your name, remove that scar. Or not, it's up to you.

'As far as your current quest is concerned, I won't hinder you. I'll do as you all ask and stay quietly at home.' The author wrote a name and number on one of Lon's opened sugar packets. 'Here's somebody who might be able to help get you near the movie. Her website got shut down, so she's filming a tell-all documentary where she follows all the Wagner people around asking impertinent questions and getting thrown out of buildings.'

Ermine read: 'Phyllis DeVillers. 310-555-5902.'

'Hey, that's the girl we told you about,' Ferd said.

J.G. got up to leave. 'Thank you all – for your lives, your stories, for making me rich, for breaking me out. I'm sorry if my books have made things more complicated. If you ever want for anything, please come see me,' J.G. said.

The table was still flabbergasted as J.G. collected her purse, finished the last few drops of her drink, and walked towards the door. Just before she reached it, she turned and said. 'One piece of advice, Barry.'

'Yes?'

'Don't give Serious your ATM card,' J.G. said. 'He calls me two or three times a week, asking for money.

She waved, turned, then walked up the stairs to the steamy street.

They sat there staring at the check, basking as if it were some sort of heat-lamp of prosperity. Eventually, Barry spoke. 'That J.G. Rollins is all right.'

It was like a spell had been broken: the group ran to the nearest bank, and deposited Barry's check.

'What now?' Ferd said, everybody's pockets full of Barry's new money.

'Not so Measly anymore, eh guys?' Barry said. 'You going to tell your parents?'

'Of course they are,' Ermine said. 'How are we going to get rid of those fans?'

'Lure them away with $1000 bills,' Jorge said, puffing on an expensive cigar. (Jorge didn't even smoke, he just felt it was appropriate, under the circumstances.)

'Forget them. We'll just stay the night in the Wizards' Club,' Barry said. 'Serious can get us some rooms.'

'As much as I am inclined to doubt every word Serious has ever, or indeed *will* ever, utter,' Ermine said. 'I need a shower, so let's go.'

To everyone's astonishment, Serious wasn't lying about the pull he had at the Wizards' Club; once the front desk had connected them to the President's office, accommodations were arranged – four rooms right next to each other on the seventeenth floor.

'You're lucky,' the bellhop said as he opened the door to Barry's room. 'There's a big oracle convention in town. These are the last four rooms left.' Barry tipped him $100. 'Wow! Thanks!' The bellhop said. 'Your buddy in the wool hat gave me a dog biscuit.'

Alone, Barry surveyed the room. It was careworn, but nice, a little musty – sort of Hogwash away from Hogwash. Prints hung on the walls, all with a magical theme; a stilted depiction of an alchemist discovering Serious Putty (no relation to Barry's godfather – or to Goo©, for that matter) hung over the bed. The furnishings were strictly academic: lots of books, big desk, small TV. Peeling off his jacket, Barry flopped on the bed, and turned on the tube.

He cruised aimlessly, and finally paused on a local public access channel. A burly gentleman in fatigues was standing in front of an American flag, fulminating about 'the mongrel races.' To hear him tell it, every human darker than a peach crayon was welded together in a conspiracy to 'enslave the Aryan race.' Even in this era of reality television, it was rare to see someone so openly insane on TV; Barry was about to change the channel when a mischievous idea popped into his head.

His wand hung in its thigh holster on the bedpost. He grabbed it and walked over to the television. Pausing for a moment to make sure he got the spell right, he waited for the moron to launch into a high-octane rush of ranting, then tapped the figure on the screen.

'Arsenio!' Barry said softly.

As quick as a belch, the man became an African-American, as dark as any son of the Congo. He continued on, unaware, becoming more ironic by the second. The horrified shout of the camera operator finally stopped him. Barry watched the fool go through anger, denial, bargaining, grief, and finally acceptance all in the space of five minutes. Barry fell asleep with the sense of a job well done.

Some hours later, the ambient noise in the room – the air-conditioning, Lon's snoring and cartoons coming from next door – fell away, revealing a tapping on Barry's window. He looked towards the grimy pane, which faced an airshaft. There stood Earwig. A squashed cigarette dangled from her beak; she had picked up the vice from watching Barry's fitful experiments with tobacco. Now she was hooked, constantly scavaging gutter-butts, tottering up to one person after another, nipping them until they gave her a light.

The window was painted shut. 'Hold on,' Barry said, jamming a letter-opener between the sill and frame,

trying to lever the window open. The opener snapped.
'Guess I'll have to break it,' Barry said aloud, giving
himself permission. He grabbed a nearby paperweight –
a bust of Bumblemore – and brought it against the glass.
The pane broke with a satisfying crunch and tinkle, as the
shards fell down the shaft. He threw the paperweight out
the window, so the Club couldn't dust it for fingerprints.

Earwig hopped in, presenting her ciggie eagerly.
Barry lit it. She was looking shabby, her snow-white
plumage stained yellow from cigarette smoke. His
familiar was an affront, an indictment, a jittery, crabby
nicotine fiend. Barry untied the messages from her foot.
He stroked her little skull absently as she buzzed and he
read the notes. The first one read:

'From Alpo Bumblemore
Hogwash School *by magic dictation pen*

Dear Barry:

I am writing to find out your progress on Plan X. Things
are getting bad here. Yesterday, two Muddles broke into the
school and scrawled profanities all over, not even having the
common decency to spell them correctly. I will not repeat the
exact words and phrases, but I assure you that they conjure
up images of enduring foulness and represent the outer
bounds of verbal depravity. They also have set several small
fires.

A small group of Muddles have taken to hanging around

Chapter Thirteen

the Buggering Birch. They seem to enjoy it, which takes all the fun out for the tree. He won't even bother you anymore. It's sad.

I have been able to keep a contingent of anti-Muddle students from taking matters into their own hands, but I am not sure I can hold them off much longer. I am not sure whether I want to.

Come in. Oh, hi, Hafwid. Some Muddles have broken into your cabin and stolen your Sacred Object?'

Barry winced. Hafwid's 'Sacred Object' – his term for it – was a ill-rendered charcoal drawing of the gigantic, teddy-clad Headmistress of Beaubeaux Academy.[12] Bumblemore did not approve of Hafwid's having it – not least because his colleague looked like a baby beluga trapped in a tuna net – but as most of the rest of Hafwid's race had been exterminated, he turned a blind eye. Anything to keep Hafwid out of the fleshpots of Hogsbleede. Barry went back to reading:

'I understand you're upset. Okay. No, I don't think killing one

[12] This was France's most prestigious magical academy, their version of Hogwash. The third major European school was a shadowy, semi-civilized place called Schadenfraude. The three periodically competed for completely meaningless awards, slaughtering tens of their students in the process. Nobody said being magical was being smart.

person a day and putting their head on stakes outside your house will get it back. They don't understand; they're an ignorant people. I'll help you. Hold on for a secI'm writing to Barry.

Barry, what is going on? Have you stopped the movie yet? If you can't do it, I think we've got a real bloodbath brewing here. The Blare Witch has offered to help – she's a Trustee – but I hope to Merlin I don't have to take her up on it. We'd be knee-deep in eviscerated Muddles and shakycam footage in no time.

Otherwise, things are pretty much as always. Hafwid says hullo, and asks, 'What do I tell the girls this week?' (??)

Hoping that – for the Love of God! – you stop this movie,
Alpo Bumblemore

PS – A group of mice are occupying the library and have taken Madame Ponce hostage. They have presented me with a list of demands. Do you know anything about this?'

Barry crumpled the letter. 'Great. He thinks it's bad now, just wait 'til the fans over there find out we're trying to stop the movie,' Barry thought, picturing colorful, Middle East-style rioting on the lawn of the school. Barry received this added pressure with all the joy of the Elephant Man being forced into a jitterbug-ging contest. Bumblemore could be overreacting. However, if he wasn't, one way or another, Barry could count on a couple thousand fewer fans in the next week or so. And if Dorco Malfeasance and all the other louts got into the action, Hogwash would soon be going toe-to-toe with the armed forces of Great Britain – and probably NATO – in no time.

Unsure of which side he would root for, Barry turned to the next letter. Earwig was standing on it, cat-like. He shooed her off, but immediately wished he hadn't read it: the letter was a demand for payment from Fuselage and Sons, for that surplus airplane he had purchased for Dali. After J.G.'s gift, he could pay this with five minutes' worth of interest. But he didn't like their tone, so Barry wrote underneath: 'Kiss my cauldron.' He refolded the letter, then motioned for Earwig to come over so that she could wing it back to England. Instead of approaching, she took two steps away and stuck out her tiny tongue; she was hungry, tired, and not going anywhere.

'I could use some food, too,' Barry said. After calling the front desk and complaining that 'a small meteor' had broken his window, he and his weary owl went downstairs to rustle up some grub. Buck yourself up, he thought. It won't do to let the others see you down. Time to be the Invincible Barry Trotter again.

Chapter Fourteen

ALL A-BORED

⟨⟩

The Club's scholastic ambience extended, unfortunately, to the food. Patrons unwise enough to dine there were confronted with standard – that is, inedible– boarding school fare. If boiled was good, fried was better, and steamed, then boiled, then fried, seemed to be their idea of culinary Nirvana. The meat was of undefined quadripedal provenance. Everything was encased in a heavy, paste-like batter, which extinguished whatever glimpses of flavour that had survived the multi-stage steaming/boiling/frying process. The daily 'specials' were just regular entrees covered with a fiercely-orange, oily, bland yet disgusting cheese, which most diners wisely avoided. Cute names masked dishes that were especially deadly; the toad-in-the-hole racked up fatalities as effortlessly and remorselessly as a machine gun.

Architecturally, the room was more pleasing.

Fashioned to look like the immense Grand Hall at Hogwash, the only thing that broke the illusion was the steady stream of New York traffic tooting outside. It was lit by chandeliers filled with flickering candles, which meant that you couldn't examine the food too closely – a small mercy. There were paintings on the walls of famous members; their severe looks suggested that each had endured a Wizards' Club meal directly before sitting for their portrait.

Such was the power of nostalgia that the Hall was constantly packed with men and women shoveling down horrible food carelessly prepared, in a drafty, poorly-lit cavern. Just like the old days, it was rowdy, too – charms being tossed around as well as food, chairs being pulled out from under people, somebody's familiar getting loose and biting the patrons, et cetera. All told, it was a thoroughly unpleasant dining experience.

By the elevators at one end, Barry saw a sorry sight – the Picking Cap, the means by which innumerable Hogwash students had been assigned houses for centuries, had been finally put out to pasture. (This was now done by a Muddle company down in London with computers, for a fraction of the cost. Picking Caps, like Italian sportscars, require lots of maintenance, and occasionally parts flown in from overseas.)

Senile, the cap sat on a chair, mumbling. 'Silverfish! No, Grittyfloor! No, wait – Pufnstuf! No . . .'

Jorge waved. The three Measlys and Ermine were sitting at a table near the waiter's station. Barry gave Earwig to the Familiar check woman to his left, and walked over.

Jorge was hitting on a pretty witch at a neighbouring table. 'My brother and I invented crop circles, you know . . . Hi, Barry! This is my friend, Barry Trotter. Perhaps you've heard of him?'

Barry left Jorge to his honey-tongued chatter and greeted the rest. 'Wow, I'm hungry,' he said.

'Well, you came to the wrong place,' Ermine said glumly. The menu was an insult to the very concept of food, and Barry ordered with an eye simply towards damage control.

'Do they eat this bad at Beaubeaux?' Ferd asked. "Vole-on-the-road?" What *is* that?'

'Breaded D-A-C-H-S-H-U-N-D, I think,' said Ermine, spelling so as not to worry Lon.

'Why are we doing this to ourselves? We're loaded,' Barry said. 'Let's go eat someplace *nice*.'

'No, Barry, we can't risk it,' Jorge said, freshly rejected. 'Someone might recognize that famous face of yours, and tear you to pieces.'

'Then can you go get takeout and bring me

something back,' Barry said, throwing down his menu. 'I eat this slop all the time at school.'

'That sounds good,' Ferd said. 'I saw a Chinese place around the corner.'

Barry gave them an order, and they headed over to Chen's – which turned out not to be Chinese at all, but Italian, run by Greeks. They hadn't gotten around to changing the sign.

Whatever its nationality, the food was tasty. They all sat on the floor of Ferd's room and ate, while Barry heard about how Ermine won $500 from a three-card monte guy outside. 'I wore my granny sunglasses,' she said. 'I could see everything. The poor fella kept thinking he was screwing up!'

'Speaking of messing with the minds of Muddles,' Jorge said, 'I called a gas leak in to Con Ed. Those fans outside our building will be gone soon enough.'

'Now that we have money, Jorge, let's get a nicer apartment,' said Ferd.

'Okay,' said Jorge. 'What are you guys going to do next?' he asked.

'Go to L.A. and find this Phyllis chick, I guess,' Barry said, through a mouthful of fried ravioli.

'I've been thinking about that,' Ermine said. 'Valu-mart obviously knows where we are and what we're doing. I think taking any magical transportation would be asking for trouble. I vote for kicking it Muddle-style.'

'Like how? Plane?' Barry asked.

Ermine remembered watching the dragons play heat-the-jet. 'I vote for train.'

'To Los Angeles?' Barry said. 'That's, like, three days.'

'Exactly. In the States, anybody who can afford to fly would never, *ever* take the train. That's why the Dork Lord would never, *ever* look for us there.'

'She's right,' Jorge said.

'Oh, God!' Barry said. There was a cigarette butt cooked into his cacciatore. He lost his appetite.

Sometime later that evening – after Lon had beaten all comers in Ping Pong – our heroes returned to their rooms. Ermine convinced the boys to stay in for the evening, to prevent alerting Dork forces to their whereabouts. 'Plus,' she added masochistically, 'we need to be at the station no later than eight a.m.!'

Making the best of a bad situation, Jorge, Barry and Lon sat in Jorge's room playing gin rummy. (Ferd was downstairs on the fifth floor, attending a 12-step group for recovering addicts of F.X. Potts' Everyflavor Legumes.) They discussed how best to get back at Zed Grimfood, and it was decided that Jorge and Ferd wouldn't come to L.A., so they could plan a proper, non-lethal, revenge. Barry noticed that the room was already a complete catastrophe – and all Jorge had done was take a nap in it. Well, Barry thought, we all have our talents.

The butterbourbon that Barry had drank with dinner to kill whatever germs were on the cigarette butt had made him sleepy. After only a few hands, and to the protestations of the Measly brothers, who were simply uncanny at the game (even Kibble-for-Brains regularly wiped him out), Barry excused himself and went to bed.

Exhausted again, Barry thought. A real job couldn't be this much work. Then he fell fast asleep.

Bright and early, Barry, Ermine and Lon trooped out of the Wizards' Club (which had magically relocated itself 20 blocks to the south) and headed for the train station. Using her credit card – 'credit is Muddle magic,' she always said – to purchase a ticket, she then used an elementary spell to issue duplicates to Barry and Lon. Serious would be proud, Barry thought.

They boarded the train, a piebald conveyance that showed every year of its age, and smelled like no window on it had ever been opened. Barry and Lon, while less offended by the aesthetics of the train, were equally annoyed by the uncomfortable chairs. Ermine immediately 'upgraded' them all to private compartments. (Anything more ostentatious would attract unwanted attention, she said.)

So Barry was ensconced in his own cozy cube, looking out of a scratched and smeary window, with his headphones blaring Valid Tumor Alarm. Their latest, 'Kill You? Sure!', had just gone platinum, and Barry picked up a copy on the way to the train station. Its raunchy lyrics and hyperaggressive beats soothed him in a way incomprehensible to the old and unhip.

As they pulled away from New York and Barry saw his last glimpse of Manhattan, he thought how much he'd like to come back to visit, preferably as a famous musician. He drowsed to the rocking movement of the train, lost in a hostile lullaby, until Ermine passed his door and gave it a rap.

Barry didn't hear, so Ermine opened it a crack and waved. Barry took his headphones off. 'What's up?' he said.

'Lon and I are going to the observation car, do you want to come?' Ermine said.

'What's that?'

'The observation car is about five cars down. It's got food and soda and tables to sit at. There's even a Plexiglas roof that you can look through – if there's anything to see, which I doubt. We're just in New Jersey.'

'I think I'll sit here for a while.'

'Suit yourself,' Ermine said, smiling, and slid the door shut.

Barry returned to the testosterone-infused babbling of Valid Tumor Alarm. 'I'm gonna cut you, cut you up good, cut your butt, like a nut would' Art Valumord screamed over a stuttering beat.

For a quasi-nymphomaniacal know-it-all, Ermine was pretty great, Barry thought. She was always doing things like seeing that Lon had a good time. I should do something nice for her, Barry decided, turning to his book. It was a thriller he had picked up in the station. This was reading of last-resort; he always found these books so unrealistic. No magic whatsoever.

Ermine had been looking out the window drinking a soda less than five minutes when a man asked if he could sit next to her.

'Sure,' she said. He was a tall, somewhat scrawny guy with close-cropped brown hair and large glasses. He had a poky Adam's apple, and one of those large, pendulous, wen-like, upper lip moles that sort of hung down and totally distracted anybody who talked to him.

'My name is Joel,' he said.

'Hi, Mo— I mean, Joel. My name is Ermine.'

'Going ALL THE WAY to L.A.?' Joel asked, emphasizing the words strangely.

'What? Yeah,' Ermine said. Definite weirdo.

'Oh, that's great. I love A LAY,' Joel said. 'BUTT IT'S HARD to spend such a LONG trip alone, isn't TIT?'

Ermine got annoyed. 'Excuse me, but what's your deal?'

'Are you turned on yet?' Joel said gleefully. 'Let's make out!'

Ermine laughed. This guy was too scrawny to pose a threat. 'Turned on by who? You?' His shirt sleeves were at least one size too long.

'Damn! Damn, damn, damn!' Joel moaned. 'I spent $1000 on a "Super Seduction" seminar, and it doesn't work at all! I'm s'posed to sprinkle "sexual words" in my conversation, and you're s'posed to get hot. But you don't! Nobody does!' He banged both his fists on the formica table between them, making a weak-sounding thump.

'Look, here's a tip from an actual, real-live girl,'

Ermine said. 'Quit with the seduction techniques, and get that gross mole removed.'

'I can't.' he said. 'I need it for business.'

Oh God, Ermine thought. The depths of Muddle craziness.

'I'm a writer, I write T-shirts. You know "Your Problem is Obvious"?'

'No,' Ermine said, keeping all enthusiasm out of her voice.

'It's the one with the cartoon of the guy with his head up his butt. It's a classic.'

'Your mother must be very proud.'

Joel bristled. 'Hey, don't laugh, I make good money. Anyway, my mole is the secret to my success. It's lucky. My lucky mole.

'I can't really explain it but, every time I've even made an appointment with a dermatologist, something bad has happened. Last time, I lost a huge account – "Ten Reasons Why a Beer is Better Than a Woman".'

'That's always struck me as particularly insulting.'

'Hey, I did "Ten Reasons Why a Cucumber is Better Than a Man," too,' Joel said defensively. 'I'm just giving the market what it wants. If Shakespeare were writing today, he'd be writing T-shirts. Who watches plays?'

'I do,' Ermine said.

'I thought you might, that's why I said it. Anyway, I lost that account, the beer versus women one. (If you're wondering, I prefer women.) Then I had a dream where my mole said, "Listen, buddy, if I go, you go." It sounds silly, but I'm not going to chance it. He sounded serious. He had a voice like a hitman.'

Barry walked by them on his way to the bar at the middle of the car. 'Hi, Erm,' he said. Who was that weird guy she was talking to? She was always such a freak magnet. Just to his right, he saw Lon hustling a group of kids in a card game. At least he wasn't the only one who Lon took money from.

'Rummy!' Lon said, 'And I'm out.'

A youthful groan went up from his opponents as Lon swept the change into a paper sack. 'Ha, ha, you lost!' he said, smoothing the moist dollar bills his ragtag opponents had fished from their socks and shoes.

'You gotta give us a chance to win our money back!' said a kid with a big nose.

'Yeah, re-tard,' another kid said, not meaning it kindly.

'No way, Jose,' Lon said, and walked over to the bar, where Barry stood. 'Bartender,' he said magnanimously. 'A kiddie cocktail for me and my friend here.' He handed the paper bag to Barry. 'Hold this.' Drink in hand, Lon went over to the table full of defeated kids and said, 'Just to show that I'm a nice guy, would you guys like some gum?'

'Sure,' Big-Nose said, and the others followed, each taking a piece of the gum. Barry watched in amazement – you could take the brain out of the Measly brother, but you couldn't take the Measly brother out of the brain.

Fiercely suppressing laughter, Lon took his drink over to where Barry sat, looking through the Plexiglas roof.

'Look at that cloud, Lon. It looks like a dragon.'

'That one looks like a circle,' said Lon, pointing at another. 'Or maybe a rectagule.'

'Rectangle. And that one over by the sun looks like a tarantula. '

'Ow! Ow!'

'Squint, Lon. Squinch up your eyes.'

'That's a lot better, Barry! Where do you learn this stuff?' Lon asked.

'Do you two gentlemen mind if I sit down?' A small man of indeterminate Asian extraction plopped down into the seat opposite them. He was completely bald, with a wispy moustache and beard. He wore lavender robes and carried a gnarled staff. Had Lon or Barry been Muddles, they would've pegged this guy for a nut

case immediately and skedaddled. But the wizarding
world is tolerant of sartorial eccentricity, sometimes to
a fault, so Barry's only thought was 'I wonder if he
knows Chi Ching?'

'Aren't the clouds beautiful?' he said, noticing what
they were doing. 'To be a cloud would be a lovely
profession.' He adjusted his lavender robes, and laid
his staff across the empty chair next to him. 'No
benefits, however, which is a problem.'

Mayhem erupted in the far corner of the train, as the
tear gas gum took effect. Lon giggled as his opponents
ran from the car, knocking over tables, thrashing
blindly towards the bathroom, choking and crying and
shrieking in pain.

'What's wrong with them?' the man asked.

'I don't know. I guess they're *re-tards*,' Lon said.
Wait a sec, Barry thought. Was Lon just *ironic*? Could
Lon be getting his sense of humor back? He used to
crack Barry up all the time, but that was before the
accident gave him a cranial breezeway.

'My name is Curtis, my friends call me Brother
Curtis, because I am a monk. I hope I can consider you
two friends?'

'Sure, Curtis,' Barry said, shaking his queerly
rubbery hand. 'Brother Curtis, I mean.'

Chapter Fourteen

'Barry, he smells like Band-Aids!' Lon said in a loud whisper.

Barry blushed, embarrassed. 'I'm sorry, you'll have to forgive my friend. He's —' then Barry mouthed the word 'developmentally-disabled.'

Curtis noddled politely. He seemed to hover slightly above his chair. 'Certainly. We must each of us follow our own path, and all of them are equally valid, even the dumb ones that lead to nowhere.'

'What's a monk?' Lon asked.

'Someone who goes off to study and pray with other people,' Curtis said.

'It's sorta like college, only for God,' Barry said to Lon. 'What type of monk are you?'

'I *was* a practitioner of Zen Buddhism. I studied and meditated for many years, hoping to find Enlightenment at a special order in Tibet, where the monks inflate themselves in an effort to float closer to Buddha. Well, it worked. Perhaps too well: when I found enlightenment, it struck me so funny that I began to laugh.

'There I was, floating and snickering, and my master said to me, "Brother Curtis, why are you laughing?"

"Existence is *hysterical*," I said.

"Fair enough," he said, and left. Twelve hours later, I was still laughing, even harder. My master came in and said, "Brother, I don't mean to be a killjoy, but nobody can meditate with your making all this racket. The goats won't eat. Plus, you're giving me the creeps."

"Plus you're giving me the creeps"? It's amazing how religious intolerance always sounds the same. "Brother, shut up or we'll call the cops!" "Brother, we're serious, shut up or we'll kick your ass!" "Brother, consider this: if we kick you out, you'll have to pay full price at the movies!" I didn't care. I laughed so loud and so long that they attached a rope to me and threw me out of my monastery, the only home I'd ever known,' Curtis said. 'I floated all the way from there to here. I'm wearing lead sandals.'

'That's a terrible story,' Barry said, with sympathy.

'Those no-minds! I'll teach them a koan or two!' Anger broke through the monk's placid surface for a moment, then receded. 'I'm going to California to start my own religion. I want to call it "Gigglism."'

'Interesting,' Barry said. 'What's a koan?'

'A koan is a question or story that forces your mind into a predicament. Zen masters – and soon, the High Yuksters of Gigglism – use them to paralyse the mind, so that they can transcend logic. If they're reverent – by which of course I mean irreverent – they'll have a gigglegasm, like I did. Would you like to hear some Gigglist koans?' Curtis asked.

'Sure,' said Barry. Lon, whose mind was in a permanent state of paralysis, stared at a bug crawling across the window.

'Okay,' Curtis said, adjusting his robe. 'Keep in mind, I just started writing them. "What is the meaning of Bodhidharma's coming from the East? Since when could *he* drive?"'

Barry stared at Curtis blankly. 'I don't know what to say.'

'Right! Aren't they great?' Curtis giggled. He leaned closer. 'A monk asked the Master Tungshan, "Who is the Buddha?" Tungshan replied, "I know you are, but what am I?"'

Barry laughed. 'Hey, that's funny. Is it supposed to be funny?'

'Definitely. All is One Big Joke.' The monk leaned still closer, smiling. Barry felt a little claustrophobic, but didn't want to be impolite. The snack guy had closed up until Denver, and the car was empty. Brother Curtis was practically sitting on Barry's lap now. His breath smelled funny – almost like helium.

'Here's my favorite, young Barry. "Joshu asked the teacher Nansen, 'Is death an end or a beginning?' Nansen thought for a moment, then replied, 'How badly do you want to know?'"'

'Wait,' Barry said. 'How did you know my name?'

Suddenly, there was a loud rushing of air and the bizarre cleric began to inflate, like a balloon, giggling maniacally. Barry and Lon scrambled to their feet and stepped away. Curtis grew larger and larger, the giggles growing to chuckles, then unhinged laughter. Soon he was so big he blocked the door at the end of the car; the pair tried the other door, but it was locked tight. 'It's a Trappist!' Barry yelled. They would be crushed! The holy man continued to expand with a menacing hiss – chairs where knocked over, tables were enveloped. Spells were useless against this creature; they bounced off it like rubber.

Brother Curtis had nearly filled the observation car; Lon and Barry were crouched at the far end of the train, pulling at the locked handle with all their strength. It was only a matter of seconds before the inflating cleric crushed them both to death.

Then Barry saw Lon take out the tiny plastic sword from his kiddie cocktail and jab it into the monk. Strange-smelling air, a mix of helium and B.O., began to rush from the hole. 'Huh?' Curtis said. Then his laughter had turned to unearthly screaming, which was so loud that Barry and Lon had to put their fingers in their ears. Soon, there was just a deflated monk lying flat on the floor. Barry nudged it with his shoe; then, sure that Curtis was no more, took it to the passageway and heaved it out the door onto the siding rolling past. '. . . and your religion was stupid, too!' Barry said, adding insult to injury.

When he returned, he saw that the observation car was pretty well wrecked; Lon was taking advantage of the destruction to get a few free bags of chips from behind the bar. 'Let's get out of here, before somebody comes and blames us for the mess,' Barry said, his voice distorted by all the helium in the air. 'Nice job, Lon.'

'Thanks,' said Lon. Maybe you're smarter than we all think, Barry wondered.

After the boys' narrow escape, our heroes decided to stay inside their compartments with the doors locked, for safety's sake. As they crossed the Great Plains, Barry could see the outlines of thunderclouds etched on the ground below. He could see the train snaking ahead, the massive engine at the front, pulling the rest. In the middle distance, Barry could see that the clouds were thicker, and darker, and could just make out rain. They were heading for the storm, and Barry was a bit excited – he felt like he was going into a car wash. Just then a flash of lightning and peal of thunder made him jump. He felt a funny feeling – could it be fear?

'Hmm,' said Barry. 'I guess this is what they mean by "foreshadowing."'

Chapter Fifteen

NIGHTMARES CAN BE EXTREMELY INSTRUCTIVE (ESPECIALLY IN CHEESY BOOKS LIKE THIS ONE)

෨෨෨

Those readers actually paying attention might wonder just what the hell is going on, to wit: 'If Barry and the gang have just left New York a few pages ago, how come they're already crossing the Great Plains? We want *magic*, not magical-realism, you knothead!'

It is a fair question. Unfortunately, it has a very unfair answer: their train was no longer a simple Muddle conveyance. It had been transformed, via that old black magic. (Cue Ermine's cell phone.) And so, the landscape that Barry saw through his dingy window was not the Plains you and I know, but a magical place were the rules of time and space and competent plotting of parodies do not apply.

The disappearance of New Jersey, Pennsylvania,

Ohio, Indiana, and Illinois was alarming, or should have been. But while the napping Ermine knew enough of American geography to have noticed the discrepancy, Barry did not – all he knew about Ohio was that Art Valumord had once been arrested for having sex with a basilisp onstage in Cincinnati.[13] And so the trio chugged along, destination DANGER!

Barry looked out the window for a while longer at the dark clouds that were getting closer and closer – they seemed to clutch at the train greedily. Barry didn't notice; lulled by the rocking of the train, he fell into a deep sleep and began to dream.

First, he dreamed that he was back in the Forsaken Forest, with his nightly contingent of groupies. They were in Barry's infamous 'Love Arboretum,' under the canopy of an immense willow tree. Things were taking their natural course, with kissing and hugging and laughing all around. Fireflies – or were they pixies committing suicide? – flickered in the cool evening air. He was chasing one particular maiden around the tree; he felt a powerful attraction to her, made more powerful by her resistance. Round and around the trunk they ran, cheered on by the others.

---

[13] To quote from J.G. Rollins' manual, *Famous Beasts and How to Prepare Them*, 'The basilisp, also called "King of the Thnakes," is excellent in a white wine sauce.'

With each circuit, Barry gained a little ground, and finally he captured his quarry. Panting and laughing, he flipped her over to kiss her – and discovered that there, on the turf beneath him, was Ermine!

'YAHHH!' Barry yelled, waking up with a start. Then, realising it was just a dream, he mumbled 'thank God' and his pulse slowly returned to normal. He shifted in his tiny bed – it was kinda cool, really compact, but really uncomfortable, too – and went back to sleep.

Unfortunately, the next dream was even more terrifying. Barry was sitting in his room at Hogwash, watching a video of Valid Tumor Alarm's latest song, 'Pistolwhippin' Infants.' The show went to commercial, and all of the sudden, there was Lord Valumart, starring in an infomercial about the benefits of the Dork Side. He was strolling around the manicured grounds of a grand estate. There were pictures of beautiful people playing golf, eating at ten-star restaurants, playing tennis, cavorting in the surf. 'And all of zem are my minions,' said Valumart, through his voluminous moustache. 'Tired of being paid less than you are vorth?' he said, pronouncing his 'w's like 'v's, as the tropical sun glinted off of the chrome spike on his helmet. 'Work for the Dork Side, and make the money that you deserve. Call zis number to find out more information.'

Suddenly, he was talking to Barry in particular: 'See zis life, Barry? See how great it is? I'm not sitting alone in my old room that smells like dirty zocks with cheesy old posters up on the vall, carving a notch into the voodvork every time I boink another Muddle. No, I'm out here in the sun and fun of L.A.!' A beach ball rolled up to Valumart's feet. He picked it up and handed it to a gaggle of bikini-clad girls. He rested a hand on his skull-headed dagger.

'Zis is my beach, Barry – zis whole thing. See how much money I have?' Valumart turned around, waving his arm to emphasize the luxury of the estate that splayed behind him. 'See vat ze Dork Side can get you, if you're just villing to grow up and get vith the program. Go for the bucks, Barry – opportunity von't vait forever. Zank you, Alicia.'

He took a tropical drink from a gorgeous waitress dressed in a thong bikini. 'Hail Lord Valumart,' she said, giggling.

'Wait for me by ze pool – I'll be taking my massage early today.' He winked lasciviously at the camera, and continued to walk down the beach.

'Do you zink your parents vould be proud if zey saw you today, Barry? A perpetual student, trading on his accidental fame to make voopie vith Muddles?' Valumart stopped, and pointed a gloved finger at him. 'I knew your parents, Barry. Of course, I killed zem, but I knew zem before I killed zem, and I don't zink zey'd like it, not one bit. Zey always hoped you'd be a lawyer.

'It's not selling out, Barry, it's buying in. You could have zis town eating out of the palm of your hand. You could create four or five long-running sitcoms before you're zrough! If you'd only join me.' He slurped his pina colada. You wouldn't think the Dork Lord would like girly drinks, but he did.

'I vouldn't vant to grow up eizer, if all I had to look forward to vas a cramped little life in zat damp little island, vith only my precious principles to keep me varm.

'No sir, make mine money. And power, yes, lots of power.'

That sounds pretty good, Barry thought.

'Join me, Barry. Ve can rule Hollywood – *as father and son*.'

What the fuck? dream-Barry thought. 'I'm not—'

'I know, I know, I just couldn't resist ripping off Darth,' Valumart said. 'He's such a sissy. Anyway, ve'll make beaucoup bucks. Come join me.'

'I vill – I mean will – join you,' dream-Barry said. And then he woke up.

Barry's dream lingered after he awoke, like a bad taste in his mouth. Was Valumart right? More importantly, did Barry, in his heart of hearts, agree with him? He got up, threw on his Army jacket, and went to the club car for some companionship. Luckily, it had been cleaned up without incident. More luckily, Ermine was sitting there, watching acre after acre roll by in the dark. She was the only one in the car; a small overhead light shone only on her booth. Barry slid into the seat opposite her, and felt a weird twinge when he realized his pal Ermine looked just like she had in his dream.

'Is the bar still open?' he said. 'Because I need a drink.'

'The guy's on break, or gone for good,' Ermine said. With his fringe, a bleary Barry brought to mind a Beatle gone bad. 'What's the matter, O Evil Moptop? Are you sick?'

'No,' Barry said. 'I just had a bad dream.'

'It's that horrible music you listen to,' Ermine said.

'No, it was Valumart. He's close – I can feel it. Listen, Ermine, maybe we should just give up,' Barry said dejectedly. 'Let them make the movie, let Hogwash close, and get on with our lives. Getting a regular job can't be as hard as this,' he said. 'I mean, look at all the idiots who have them.'

Ermine, who had a real job, was momentarily miffed. But since she was by far the most mature person in this story, she put that aside. She was shocked to see Barry, her comrade in so many battles, talking of defeat. 'We can't give up now, Barry,' she said. 'For one thing, I've used up three whole vacation days. For another, I think we're going to beat him. We always do.'

'But what if we can't stop the movie, and Hogwash has to close?'

'Well, then, you get a real job. It's not that bad being an adult, really. But we have to give it our best shot. That's worth something.'

'I guess, but what if the movie really *sucks*?'

'We can't think like that,' Ermine said. 'We'll shut the movie down somehow. There's that klieg light, for one thing.'

Barry began to feel better. 'Erm,' he said, 'why haven't you and I ever dated?' The lust he felt in his dream was welcomed back like a conquering hero. Consulting his copy of *Lies Men Tell Women*, he said, 'Don't worry – if things didn't work out, we would still be friends.'

'I've said this before, you're not my type,' Ermine

said. Actually, the real reason was that Barry's glasses made him look freaky – one eye was farsighted, the other near, which gave him one huge googly eye and one tiny, beady one. It had always unnerved Ermine just enough to prevent any attraction from taking hold. And, earlier, when they'd first met, there had been his intermittent commitment to hygiene. Still, maybe someday . . . but not now. Quoting her copy of *Lies Women Tell Men*, she said, 'You know what they say, "Girlfriends come and go, but friends are forever."'

'Like a really ugly tattoo you got when you were drunk.'

'Yes, exactly,' Ermine said, laughing. 'Now that you're rich, I hope you'll be less of a jerk,' she said. 'Nothing to prove. You can just be yourself now, right?'

'I don't know,' Barry said. 'I've been acting like Mr. Famous Invincible for so long, I don't know if I can stop. I don't know if there's a myself to be.'

Ermine thought for a moment, then said, 'There's a spell for that. Want me to cast it?'

'A spell for what?'

'To allow you to be yourself, all the time, no matter what,' she said. 'I learned it in seventh year, while you were cutting classes and ingesting substances.' She got out her wand.

'I don't know, Ermine. I'm a little . . .'

'Sh.' Ermine started to speak rapidly in a low whisper. Her wand traced bizarre shapes in the air, the tip giving off a faint trail of luminescence. Then there was a small pop.

'Okay, you're done,' she said.

Barry felt a calm pass over him. 'Wow, Erm. I already feel different.'

'Good.' There was no spell, but if Barry thought there was, it would work all the same. 'Now go back to bed. We're getting into L.A. bright and early, and you need to be fresh. Plus' – she looked at her watch – 'my new friend should be here any minute.'

Barry got up. He leaned over the table and gave Ermine a hug. 'Thanks. For the spell. And the friendship.' He tried not to cop a feel, but old habits die hard.

'You're welcome,' Ermine said, not minding. She checked her watch, which glowed in the twilight of the dimmed car. 'Now, scram.'

'Amazing,' Barry said, shaking his head. 'Ermine, is there anybody who *doesn't* give you a moistie?'

'Hey, watch it,' Ermine said, offended. 'At least I don't do groupies.'

'It was kind of a compliment. You're a far cry from the shy, bookish lass I met all those years ago.'

Ermine smiled, a little sheepishly. 'How are you supposed to know what's good if you don't sample the buffet?'

Barry laughed. 'Happy hunting,' he said, and walked up the aisle. As he walked through the sliding door, he bumped into a man rushing in the opposite direction. It was Moel.

'Sorry,' he said. Barry chuckled as he walked back to his compartment.

Since it was dark, there was nothing to do but sleep, but since Barry had just slept, all he could do was drift in a half-awake haze. Time passed, the miles rolled by. He was knocked into consciousness by the conductor's voice as he walked down the hallway. 'Las Vegas station in five minutes, Las Vegas.'

His interrobang throbbed, and Barry swallowed an aspirin; maybe it was the legalised prostitution. He sat there, trying to think the pain away. There was something familiar about that conductor – seemed like a rougher character than you'd expect on Amtrak. The gapped smile ... the scarred nose and face ... Suddenly, Barry remembered: it was the same man that had ushered him into the faulty toboggan back in

Chapter Three! 'Crikey! I should tell Erm about this,' Barry said to himself. (He could tell *Lon* too, but it wouldn't matter.)

Speaking of, Lon stuck his head in the door. 'Barry, that guy that you like is getting on the train.'

'Which guy, Lon?' he said impatiently. His headache wasn't going away, it was getting worse.

'That singing guy.'

Singing guy, singing guy . . . 'Raffi? John Tesh?'

Lon nodded "no." 'Art Somebody.'

'You don't mean Art Valumord? The guy from Valid Tumor Alarm? NO WAY!' All previous thoughts – and headaches – had been swept away by the unreasoning power of Barry's fandom.

Barry immediately began spinning fantasies. He would go back and meet Mr. Valumord. They would hit it off right away, after he realized that Barry, too, belonged to that mystical brotherhood forged by raw talent. They'd joke, laugh, maybe he'd offer Barry one of his 'ladies.' Then, as night turned into dawn, Mr. Valumord (who by now Barry would call by his street handle, 'Old Smelly Bastard') would ask Barry to sit in on his next album. Barry would feign embarrassment, but Mr. Valumord would plead, saying his career depended on it, and finally Barry would consent to leading Valid Tumor Alarm for the next tour and beyond.

The train gave a slight lurch, as Art's personal car was attached. As any fan knew, VTA's frontman had sworn off flying after getting food poisoning from an airline meal. (One might suggest that he simply swear off airline food, but such were the quirks of genius.) It was all Barry could do to resist charging back there immediately, but even in his fan-fogged state, he thought he'd give Art a chance to collect himself, ready himself for the arrival of his heir apparent. Barry sat, fidgeting and checking his appearance in the mirror.

Finally, our hero couldn't stand it anymore, and sprang up. He walked down the hall so quickly that the creepy conductor yelled at him to stop running. Barry waited for the door to close behind him, then ran more, out of spite. He arrived at the door to the car slightly out of breath.

Just as Barry was about to knock, it slid open.

'I've been expecting you,' a familiar voice said.

Chapter Sixteen

RELAX, IT'S LATER
THAN YOU THINK

ᏈᎥᎥᏈ

Barry stepped inside the custom-made car, which was easily as long as a regular passenger coach, and covered with carpeting so deep and soft that his weak ankle gave way. 'Ow!' he said, hopping to a chair.

'Take your shoes off, I don't want you messing up my carpet,' Art called from the next room, causing Barry to frantically retrace his hops and slip off his ratty sneakers. 'There's malt liquor in the fridge, make yourself at home. I'm in the bathroom, I'll be out in a second.' Barry could hear vacuous high-pitched giggles.

He looked around. It was, for all practical purposes, Heaven. The lights were low; there were candles, which made the tiger-print wallpaper dance hypnotically; posters of bikini-clad women (autographed with the models' own childish scrawls: 'To Art, the best I ever had') hung on the walls, along with VTA's spate of gold and platinum records.

In one corner, there was a fully-stocked bar, with a state-of-the-art sound system behind it, pumping out VTA's latest hit, 'Sugar, Sugar,' a sassy remake of the old bubblegum hit with plenty of phat beats and swearing. In the other corner, there was a long black leather couch. A huge, flat-screen TV was swung down from the ceiling, airliner-style, and played 'Scarface.' It was rumored that Valumord was funding a shot-by-shot remake of the movie, and providing the soundtrack. Barry tiptoed over to the couch and sat down to watch.

'All of you wait for me in there,' Barry heard Art say. The bathroom door swung open, and there he was, Barry's Maximum Leader, in a leopard-skin silk bathrobe. He was scrawny but tough-looking; his pale skin was covered with tattoos (both professional and self-inflicted) that were said to be evil runes in a language he made up. His dyed purple hair was spiky short, and shaved on the sides, with the stubble dyed pink. His teeth were bad enough to make a third-world dentist gag. He was equal parts Jim Morrison, Sid Vicious, and Elton John. And Barry *idolized* him, truly, madly, deeply. Art was ugly, his music was ugly, but –

as Barry had pointed out during many an argument with unbelievers – life was ugly, too.

'Hi, Barry, sorry you had to wait,' Art said. 'I had some . . . business to attend to.' He wiped his nose and walked over to the bar. 'Can I get you anything? Tequila? Courvoisier?'

Barry was much too nervous to drink, but he didn't want to come off like a wuss. 'Do you have a beer?'

'Sure, Barry. It's good to pace yourself. We've got a long night ahead.'

This confused Barry, but it sounded promising, so he smiled.

Art handed Barry a beer and sat down on the couch next to him. 'Cheers,' he said, and threw down a shot – something strong, by the way he squinched his face up.

'What do you think of my crib-away-from-the-crib?' Art asked.

'It's great,' Barry said.

'Oh, come now, Barry, you can be honest. What's the point of being old friends if they can't be honest?' Art poured himself another shot.

'Old friends? Mr. Valumord, I have all your CDs, I think I would remember if we had met!'

Art turned the TV off; the music still blared. 'Now, Barry, that's only your first beer. Look at me. Concentrate,' Art said. 'You *sure* you haven't seen me before?'

Barry was perplexed. He wanted to say 'yes,' since that was so obviously what Art wanted to hear, but couldn't.

'God, you are dim! I can't believe you've caused me so much trouble.' Art slammed the shotglass down on the table, causing whatever was it to splash onto the carpet. He stood up. 'Look!'

Art took off his bathrobe, and instantly – magically – he began to change. His frail, scribble-filled chest turned into a tunic full of medals, with a skull-topped dagger and a crimson sash at the waist; his spindly, junk-food nourished legs turned into sinister black jodphurs, with knee-high shiny boots and vicious spurs; on his lip a walrus moustache began to sprout; and his multicolored mop of damaged hair disappeared under a black and silver helmet topped with a gleaming spike.

'Oh my God,' Barry said. 'You're Lord Valumart! Or Nunnally!'

'You vish,' Valumart said.

Barry was shocked. 'But how? When did you . . .'

Valumart made an impatient gesture. 'Dork magic. It vas easy.'[14]

---

[14] *Author's note*: This is Valumart's big chapter, but a little pidgin

'Wait a sec,' Barry said suspiciously. 'If you're Lord Valumart, why isn't my scar hurting?'

'I figure that your parents got sick of you ignoring it, and took it away. You're like somebody who takes all the batteries out of their smoke detectors, then whines when their house burns down,' Valumart said. Barry looked in the mirror and lifted his fringe; sure enough, *the mark was gone.*

'What a dummy you are, Barry – whenever your scar hurt, all you had to do was go tell Bumblemore . . . at least in the days before he started hitting the potion cabinet. But you always had to solve the mystery,' Valumart said mockingly. 'I wasted years trying to kill you, when I could've just left you alone. Your pathetically-bad judgment would've gotten you arrested or killed, and I would've been free to concentrate on my music.'

'Hold on: so you really *are* Art Valumord?'

'*And* Valid Tumor Alarm.'

'No way, no way!' Barry said.

'Way. Rearrange the letters,' Valumart said. 'I will wait.' He turned on the TV and began watching the massively-popular *Amateur Hospital.*

German goes a long vay – er, way. So I'm going to write it normally, but whenever Valumart speaks, imagine him with a ridiculous, vaudeville-quality Teutonic accent. Now, back to the book.

An embarrassingly long time later, Barry held up a scratch pad. 'Art Valumord doesn't spell Lord Valumart!' he said indignantly.

'Middle initial is "L",' Valumart said without taking his eyes off the screen. Barry jumped to his feet. 'You *are* Lord Valumart!' He reached for his wand. It wasn't there.

'In your haste to meet your hero, you left your weapon behind,' Lord Valumart chuckled. 'For someone so plagued by fans, it is ironic, no?' He turned to Barry. 'Anyway, commence with the relaxing. *You* summoned *me*, remember?'

'No, I didn't!'

'Oh, but you did,' Valumart said. 'Watch.' He pushed a button on his remote, and a bumbling, D.I.Y. colonoscopy was replaced by a picture of Barry asleep in his compartment. 'I vill – I mean will – join you,' the figure mumbled. 'You said it, I didn't,' Valumart said.

Barry was poleaxed. Several times, he opened his mouth to speak, then closed it after nothing sensical came to mind. As Barry sat there dazed, Valumart walked over to the wall, and pulled down an organizational chart titled 'Valumart Enterprises.'

'In 1960, while exiled in Argentina, I invented the concept of "muzak." And from that one invention – helping along by some highly questionable business practices – this mighty holding company was born.' In addition to the media empire – which ranged from over thirty distinct flavors of stomach-churning porno to yes, *Amateur Hospital* – the Dork Lord had extensive interests in credit cards, pesticides and food additives, institutional catering, arms dealing, and modern architecture.[15] If it was shady, shoddy, or deadly, Valumart Enterprises made it.

'Behold the Valumart octopus,' he said, proudly. 'We don't make the elevators, we make them *slower*. We don't make the toilet seats, we make them *colder*. You get the picture.' He chuckled, and shut his pointer. 'Get a load of this latest slogan: "Valumart Enterprises: The Irritation Company."'

'Wow,' Barry said. For the first time in all of his adventures, he finally saw the extent of Lord Valumart's power. Trying to buck himself up, he said insolently, 'If you're so rich and powerful, why do you talk like Colonel Klink from *Hogan's Heroes*?'

'You are English, and to the English, the Germans are still the ultimate stock villain. If you were Mexican, I would be American. Indian, Pakistani; Israeli, Arab. Whichever nationality you hold the most prejudice

[15] In fact, he owned Taste Sensations, the company Ermine pretended to work for. Oh, the delicious irony!

towards, I will be. It helps me maintain the proper level of hostility.'

Valumart picked up his leopard-print bathrobe and folded it. 'Anyway, what's to think about? Come let me make you rich, famous, loved beyond your wildest dreams.'

'But I'm already rich and famous,' Barry said.

'That's as wild as your dreams get? A few million pounds and plenty of Clearasil on the hoof?' Valumart said. 'Wait 'til you have your own line of clothes, or get caught smuggling an AK-47 into the Grammys, or talk about your aspirin addiction on Okrah,' Valumart said. 'That's *real* fame, book boy. You haven't even begun to scratch the surface of it. Join me – we can cut a single this afternoon. I'll call up Poop Dogg.'

Oh, it was terribly tempting . . . A moment passed, then Barry turned to his old enemy and said, 'I won't do it.'

Valumart's face contorted into a mask of rage. 'You – you – YOU WELCHER!' he shouted. The giggles from the other room abruptly stopped. 'I turned down a sweet gig at Caesar's Palace to come out here and get you!'

He goosestepped angrily around the room, sweeping things off counters and tables, hurling chairs. Soon the car looked like a rolling version of Ferd and Jorge's

Chapter Sixteen

apartment. 'I should have known! You've always been a self-absorbed, immature, Muddle-loving twerp!' Barry noticed that Valumart stayed between him and the door at all times. With Lon and Ermine, he would've had a fighting chance, and Valumart knew it.

Finally, Valumart regained his composure; he straightened himself, smoothed his moustache, and said calmly, 'Ah, well. Now we commence with the killing.'

Valumart whipped out his wand – which, like his dagger, had a smiling skull on the end of it – and pointed at the ground. There was an earsplitting bang and everything disappeared in billows of heavy, purple smoke.

When Barry regained consciousness, he was strapped at wrist and ankle to an upright stone slab in a dank, gloomy dungeon. Rats scurried along the walls; cobwebs were everywhere. (Ensorceled spiders had weaved them into letters reading, 'Welcome Back!' and 'World's Greatest Boss.') There, in the corner, were a row of small coffins, rudely hewn from the living rock.

Valumart stood before him, tapping his wand against his palm. '*Guten tag*, Barry,' he said. 'Welcome to my new home in the south of France. Too bad you're going to have such a short visit, or else I'd show you around.

It was once a swinging crash pad for the Knights Templar.

'Upstairs, there's a monastery, where monks make 900-proof brandy,' Valumart said. 'It's good. I hear Hafwid likes it.' Valumart's spies were everywhere, Barry thought.

'Yes, they are,' Valumart replied. 'I can hear your thoughts, Barry, but you can't cast any pesky spells . . . Tsk, tsk – what a dirty mouth you have. Don't judge the place so harshly. This is just the basement work area – it's been used for torture for over 1000 years. I bought it from George Harrison. You wouldn't believe the horrid wood panelling he had put up.

'Forgive me if I sit. I am not as young as yourself.' Valumart sat in a papasan chair rudely hewn from the living rock,[16] and continued to talk.

Next to Barry, a small dehumidifier, R.H.F.T.L.R., whirred. 'You will notice, Trotter, that evaporation would be useless. You would escape your bonds, yes, but die in the moistureless, mechanical guts of this machine.' Valumart grinned, patting it. 'It keeps the place from getting moldy. These medieval torture chambers are so damp.'

Valumart unsheathed his wand. 'You've been a

[16] Hereafter abbreviated as 'R.H.F.T.L.R.'

worthy adversary, so I'm going to give you the James Bond Special. First, you'll be interested to know what happens to Lon and Ermine.' White smoke spread itself all over the opposite wall, until it resembled a screen, then twin silver beams shot from the skull's eyes on the tip of Valumart's wand.

'No, I'm not going to make you watch *Scarface* again. Always with the quips,' Valumart turned to the screen, and the images began to move. He cleared his throat and began to speak. 'Okay, so – after you die, your friends see the errors of their ways and join me.'

Barry saw Ermine dressed in beautiful clothes, in business meetings, ordering people around. 'Yes, I too am glad she didn't marry Nunnally. He wouldn't have been good for her, and made it slightly more difficult for me to marry her myself.'

Barry screamed. Valumart winced. 'I would ask you to stop with the screaming. You are deafening me in my brains. They say that behind every evil genius bent on world domination, there is a great woman. Well, Barry, they are right. So, so right.'

The screen went milky for a moment, then a picture of *Attainment Weekly* spun into focus, revealing Lon's tanned face smiling confidently. 'That 62 IQ finally paid off for Lon – he has a successful career in television programming. Lon becomes one of the most powerful men in the industry – second to me, of course.'

Valumart waved his wand again, and the screen dissipated.

'Now, on to Part Two of killing your enemy courteously: I have to tell you my plan.'

Barry looked over at the coffins. 'You are correct. That will be your final resting place. Sort of. Those coffins are where I keep the souls of children's books, after I remove them and turn them into bland big-budget films. Your body will exist, but your soul – the part of you that makes you unique, and so crazy uncontrollable – will be in here, in this coffin. I admit, if you had joined me, the same thing would've happened, but at least you would've profited a bit from the process.

'For as long as we've fought, Barry, I've been getting stronger – you have no idea how much I spend on marketors! You and your pals never had a chance.' He-Who-Smells paused, basking. 'I'm everywhere. I'm the guy who makes you pay $17.99 for a CD that costs $1 to make. I'm the chemicals in your food. I'm advertising, air pollution, and cheap-ass workmanship. I'm sweatshops. product placement, shameless tie-ins, and hype. I empty heads and fill landfills.'

Jesus, Barry thought. I've never been more bored in my life. Hurry up and kill me, already.

'Patience, Barry. The killing part is coming. But, as powerful as I am, I have a problem. Some people can still tell the difference between good stuff and crap. Not a lot of people – fewer all the time – but some. So, I decided I had to get at them before they can resist me. I had to win their loyalty *as children*. That's where you come in.'

Valumart paused. 'Of course it's fiendish, Barry. *I* thought of it. Now pay attention, I want to kill you and go have something to eat. I skipped dinner for that nonsense on the train.' A rat scuttled from the shadows and began to gnaw on Barry's sock. A vaporous fist shot from Valumart's wand, and bonked it on the noggin. The rat reared up on its back legs and grabbed its head in pain and confusion. 'No, not yet, Agent X-13,' Valumart said. 'Please forgive my associate.

'After my last defeat I had a brainstorm: instead of wasting any more years fighting you, why not use you as bait for all those young, impressionable minds? The Trotter, movies – yes, there will be many – will replace the books. You will look how I want you to look, say what I want you to say, act how I want you to act. Your fans will forget the decent youngster in the books and remember only the saccharin numbskull I create!'

Valumart got up and started to walk around; his excitement was too much to contain. 'Kids all over the world will pay good money to see their hero, Barry Trotter, defeat bad old Lord Valumart. Little do they know that every dollar, yen and rupee they pay will make me more powerful! And the cheesy tie-ins, the shameless promotions – all that money will go to me, too!'

Valumart put his face right in Barry's, so close that his breath steamed up Barry's glasses. 'I'm going to extract every last dollar from you! I'm going to do it so shamelessly and ruthlessly that eventually even your biggest fans will puke. I'm going to make them *hate* you, Barry Trotter!'

Valumart regained his composure. 'To answer your question, the movie is pretty darn good. Not as good as the books, but "an unforgettable piece of holiday cine-magic." You see, I already have the blurbs written.'

But here is the masterstroke: each sequel will be a little bit worse, a little bit more slapdash, a little bit stupider. Have you ever seen *Jaws 4*? That will make *Barry Trotter 4* look like *Hamlet*. Finally, the series will get so incredibly bad that nobody will want to see it, but they'll be forced to, by a misguided sense of completeness or the whining of their own brats, who won't know any better. And why should they? For all of their young lives, the Barry Trotter movies have been there. They will be beyond "bad" or "good" they will simply be a part of everybody's childhood. Nostalgia is a powerful thing – ever eaten at the Wizards' Club?

'There will be Barry Trotter wands, robes, brooms, figures, board games, stationery, pens, candy, T-shirts, coffee cups, calendars, audio books, stones, trading cards, comics (manga, alternative and regular), theme restaurants, an amusement park, a video game – and maybe a hockey team, if I can find enough Russians. The kids will have stickers and party favors and shampoo that cleans your hair "magically" but is really the same old crap in new bottles. Mom gets Earwig earrings, Dad gets the Trotter edition SUV. I'm so dastardly I can't stand it!

'And I'll take every penny and turn it into scores of dumb TV shows, boring books, mindless video games . . . Their minds will turn to glop, so full of my dreck that they won't even be able to *imagine* life being any different. Pity the poor Muddles, Barry. Imagination is the only magic they have – and you're going to help me take it from them!'

Valumart paused a moment, his eyes shining, leaning against a ballet barre R.H.F.T.L.R. 'Excuse me. I always get a little choked up when I think about it.' He turned to Barry, and walked towards him. He put his wand directly over Barry's heart.

'Ah, well,' Valumart said firmly: 'Prepare to go to the Big Remainder Table in the Sky, Barry Trotter.'

Just then, a voice yelled, 'CUT!'

Chapter Seventeen

YES, ADULTHOOD
STINKS, BUT CONSIDER
THE ALTERNATIVE

omuo

'Perfect, Mel, just perfect,' the director said.

'Jesus, overact much?' the actor playing Barry said, as a stage hand unstrapped him.

'Are we okay?' said the director to several people at once. Getting an affirmative from sound and lighting, he said, 'Ladies and gentlemen, that's a wrap.' The crowd, mostly crew but also bigshots like Barry, clapped and cheered.

Chloe, the production assistant came up to Barry, who was sitting behind the director, as an honored guest. 'What did you think?' she said. 'Did we do it justice?'

'Sure,' said Barry, who had nodded off for Takes 17-27. 'The real Valumart swears a lot more, but I understand it's a kids' movie. I'd like to see the ending,' he said. 'Valumart loses, of course?'

Chloe returned his smile. 'Of course. Barry survives – the tube of loyal jelly in his breast pocket absorbs the death spell – but he's very weak. When Lon and Ermine realize that Barry is no longer on the train, they do the anagram and alert Bumblemore. Using enchanted copies of the *Financial Times*, he lures Valumart into an abandoned phosphorous mine, then sends Sparky the phoenix in on a suicide mission.'

'Ouch!'

'Yeah. Beautiful explosions. And the THX will make your ears bleed. But that's all I'm going to say – you'll just have to see it to find out the rest, Mr. Trotter.'

'Call me Barry, please.'

She handed him a videotape. 'All right, Barry. Here's a "rough cut" of the movie – it's got everything but what you saw today.' She wagged her finger at him. 'Now don't you put this up on the net or anything – it's top secret.'

Barry laughed. 'I won't, I promise.'

The actor playing Barry approached the real thing. 'Barry, I'm a big fan,' he said. 'I hope you enjoyed being on the set.'

'I'm a big fan of yours, too, Jimmy,' Barry said genuinely. 'I'm glad they let you out of rehab to do the picture.'

'I'm not so sure it isn't this business that makes me

want to do drugs in the first place,' Jimmy said
wearily. Jimmy Thornton was around 20, looked 40,
but filmed 15. He had a reputation for unreliability, a
mean temper, and a raging substance-abuse problem.
Some people didn't approve of him playing Barry, but
he brought a Brando-like intensity to the character that
the real Barry loved. *He actually knees Valumart in the
nuts,* Barry thought with relish. *As if!*

'Anyway, I'll see you at the wrap party tonight?'
Jimmy asked.

'Afraid not,' Barry said. 'I have to fly back to England
tonight.' He was giving another talk, 'Muddles, Magic,
and Me,' for a group in London tomorrow. It was good
money, but God, was it boring.

'Sorry to hear that,' Jimmy said, removing his wig.
Barry noticed that Jimmy was balding, with follicles
now numbering only in the hundreds. *He might have
been naïve, but it never failed to amaze Barry when
actors didn't look the same in real life.*

'Can I walk you to your car?' Chloe said. Like any
well-trained underling, she had kept her distance while
the money players had networked.

'Sure,' said Barry. 'See ya, Jimmy.'

They exited the building into the bright California
sun. Barry immediately put on his sunglasses. *Can't
understand why people go bonkers over this weather,*

he thought. Too bright, no variety, good for a cactus but not for a man. Whenever he was out there, he always thought of his great-great-uncle, who died of heatstroke fighting for Empire in the Sudan. Barry had just turned down a cushy gig as a 'greeter' at a Vegas casino, a swords-and-sorcery themed joint named Camelot's Castle. It was hard to say no to $50,000 a week, but he didn't need the money, and besides, the desert sun would bake his brains but good.

'Thanks,' he said, as the burly driver opened the limo door.

'Well . . . I hope you enjoy the movie,' Chloe said.

'I'm looking forward to it. I love a good explosion.'

Barry didn't pay much attention to his driver's dreams of becoming a guitar hero, because he had agreed to participate in an online chat, to promote the movie.

Host: I'd like to welcome a very special guest this afternoon to Yowser.com. The one and onley Barry Trotter! Please send your questions to him now.

GemstonePaul: I thot u were dead

Host: For the LAST TIME, the 'clues' on the book covers are total rubbish. Barry is fine.

Exciteable1: BARY RULEZ!!!!!!!!!

BT: Thanks!

Trotfan24: in *Scary Magical Whatever*, when U R fighting the vomyt wyrm, and the spiret of your parents emerge from the Spigot of Souls to save u, y is your mom wearing a crimson toga when in *Scone* it clearly states that she was wearing a crimson-edged WHITE toga when Valumart killed her? There is a bet riding on this.

BT: You'd have to ask J.G., I didn't write the books.

Trotfan24: cop out

BT: The vomyt wyrm was modeled after an encounter I had with an amazingly hostile and persistent garden slug. Hafwid killed it by breathing on it

Host: Wow! Heard it here first, fans!

BT: Also, as I have said many times, Terry Valumart did not kill Mum & Dad. True, he made the bomb that they were planting in the Chemistry building – for reasons that are unclear, but must've made sense back in the 60s. I suspect 'the Man' was invoked passionately and often. Anyway, Terry was stoned, but it wasn't like he TRIED to kill them. Being a revolutionary is a dangerous job.

Host: From revolutionary to Finance Minister! He-Who-Smells has certainly changed over the years!

BT: The fringes are always closer together than you think. Anyway, Mum and Dad and Terry were all in the 'Sports and Weather Underground' together.

Teetz9: So M&D were hippys?

BT: Yes. I was raised in a commune in Sussex. Lots of nudity and Donovan.

Derek937: WASSUP!!!!!!!!!!!!!

DynaMatt: Valumart's first name =Terry?

BT: Terence. He hates it. That's why he's 'Lord' now. But everybody used to call him 'He-Who-Smells' back on the farm. No running water.

Host: So, Barry: what have you done in the five years since the real Hogwash closed?

BT: For a while I just slacked. Then I got involved with my Uncle Serious running a company that magically turns crayfish into lobsters for the Muddle market. That's on hold until Serious gets out of Aztalan.

Teetz9: Ouch

BT: No, it's fine. He's kind of a celebrity. Now, I travel around giving a talk called 'Magic, Muddles and Me.'

Trollx78: I thought u were rich. Y do u work

BT: Because otherwise I'd become a great pudding!

Host: Have you seen the new movie? What do you think?

BT: This movie will be hailed as one of the greatest achievements of

Barry paused, and fished in his mouth with an index finger that tasted of plastic and keyboard grime. Sure enough, there was a chip under his tongue. Never should've eaten in the Wagner Bros. commissary,

Barry thought, and pitched it out the window. He deleted his earlier response.

Derek937: WASSUP!!!!!!!!!!!!

Host: Have we lost you, Barry?

BT: Sorry. I just got back from the set. It's cool. I think people will like it.

Host: What's it about, for people who don't know?

BT: Me, Lon, and Erm try to stop a movie from being made about me.

Host: Which you really did, right?

BT: Yes. But all I did in real life was write a letter or two.

Trollx78: Barry T and the Querulous Postmistress.

BT: LOL

Teetz9: I've been hearing abot this 4 years. Y did it take so long to get made.

BT: It's actually the SECOND shot at a movie. The first one was based on the books, and died in development hell. Kubrick was going to do it, but died of beard poisoning. Martin Scorsese was excited until J.G. told him he couldn't set it in Little Italy in the 70s. Then the money fell through – Serious took it, which is why he's in jail now. At that point, nobody thought a Trotter movie would ever get done. My agent tried all the spells she knew, but money's more powerful than magic. In Hollywood at least!

Host: So how did it happen?

BT: I was visiting J.G. at her Carribbean retreat in Scotland, and we had an idea to write ANOTHER movie, this one based on trying to stop the FIRST one.

Host: Whoa. Meta. The second one is about a first movie that never got made?

BT: Yeah. I had the experiences five years ago, J.G. and I wrote the screenplay three years ago. Then the Farrelly brothers optioned it and it's been in production ever since.

Viagratrix: Were a lot of liberties taken with the real story?

BT: As always. For example, J.G. Rollins wasn't held hostage by Fantastic. She just had a very restrictive contract.

Viagratrix: So it's metaphorical.

BT: I think it's not as much metaphorical as a bunch of hacks sitting in a room making shit up.

Host: Are you angry?

BT: It's not the movie I would've made. Everybody's always farting and throwing up. It's crude. I guess they just didn't have the skill or imagination to do it another way . . . I just don't understand why some people think bodily functions are so funny. It seems to me like a case of arrested development. But everyone in Hollywood seems to be ten years old.

ToyGal21: Do u long to tell yr real story.

BT: God, NO! Contrary to what people expect, I have a pretty boring life. I do a little magic every once in a while, mostly to avoid something I don't wanna do. But the usual is watching TV or hanging out at the pub. Normal stuff.

Host: So the Barry Trotter we know and love is a complete fiction?

BT: I lead a very average existence. Like most of us – that's why we need books and movies.

Mdlhtr80: Do you hate mudles?

BT: Of course not! Some of my best friends etc

ToyGal21: Are you married

BT: Engaged.

Host: WHOA! More breaking news! To whom, Barry?

BT: I'd rather not say.

ToyGal21: TEL ME WHO BARRY I'LL KILL HER

Derek937: WASSUP!!!!!!!!!!!!!

Host: you are an idiot

Derek937: get stuft WASSSUP!!!!!!!!!!

BT: And WASSUP to you, my friend

GinaB: I luv Carson Daly he is the #1 best

ElfSammy: Sam and Kaitlyn TLF

Mdlhtr80: Kaitlyn is a MUDDLE

ElfSammy: shut up you trollfu—

Barry stopped reading and closed his laptop; clearly the mob had taken over the chat. He was tired of it anyway. He closed his eyes and dozed while his driver droned on. 'I remember the first time I heard Jimmy Page, man – I knew what I wanted to do with my life! That freaky double-necked guitar . . .'

As the limo approached LAX, the driver looked through the rear-view mirror, into the back seat. Making sure that Barry was fast asleep, the driver suddenly wrenched the wheel, and let out a bloodcurdling howl: 'Death to the Trotter! Long Live Valumart!'

Barry jumped awake. The driver was ululating incoherently as the limo leaped the median, and barreled towards oncoming traffic. There was no time to do anything but escape; he had learned to keep the window open a crack at all times, for just such emergencies. With a quick incantation, Barry evaporated.

Now a sentient cloud of damp, Barry watched from a safe distance as the cars scattered. The limo somehow made it through the traffic, broke through the airport fence, and careened down a runway. The driver, thinking that Barry was still in the back seat, searched for a lethal enough destination: he found it in a truck reading 'DANGER: JET FUEL.' Barry saw it, and cast a fast-acting spell:

'Nerfere!'

the tanker truck was instantly transformed into soft pink foam rubber. The limo slammed into it, and bounced off harmlessly. The driver, puzzled, leaped from behind the wheel and began flinging himself against the truck, determined to perish somehow. But the soft surface just bounced him back gently, until he finally gave up and sat on the ground, weeping.

'It's okay, buddy,' Barry heard a cop say as they arrested him. 'Come with us.'

What can you do with an idiot like that? Barry thought, watching the action serenely from above, coasting on a zephyr. Once a month or so, some Earth Eater who never got the memo from Headquarters tried to do Barry in. He wafted over to the terminal and disevaporated. 'Great – now my suit smells like mildew.'

High over the Atlantic trying not to think of the aeronautical ramifications of Murphy's Law, Barry was busy chewing over what the movie's version of Terry Valumart had said. He'll be happy that they left out his stutter, Barry thought.

Several years ago, Valumart got arrested for tax-evasion, but had landed on his feet as usual: he pulled a plea-bargain and turned all his followers in. He retired to Bermuda, started giving a lot of money to the Tories. When they got in, they made Valumart Finance Minister. He had just (ghost) written an autobiography – *Cheaters Prosper!* – that called Barry and his cohorts 'ignorant, youthful anarchists.' Barry didn't know whether to be offended or pleased.

Taking airplanes always made Barry pensive – perhaps it was the fumes. He thought about the chat, how easily he slipped back into that fakey Invincible Barry persona he always used around fans. Ermine should've never told him the spell she cast was a placebo.

Why did he say that his life was boring these days, when it ran him ragged? Sure, keeping a low profile was good; he didn't want every two-bit teen wizard with something to prove, barging in wand blazing when he was on the loo. (This had actually happened.) But it was more than that – he was embarrassed because his life no longer made interesting reading. I'm working as hard as I ever did saving the world, just trying to be a decent person, Barry thought. It was depressing: was this all he could do?

Ermine always told him, 'Your life isn't a book, nobody's is. Look for the heroism in everyday things. Try staying married without strangling each other, or raising kids who aren't total psychopaths – it's not glamorous, but it's just as difficult as whalloping an Irish Whiskeybreath with a wicked hangover.'

She was so wise, it was annoying. Still, there were times that he wanted to return to Hogwash, and the carefree life he once had. That first movie may have died in Development Hell, but it took his good old days along with it.

Another chat lie: he really did try to stop the movie, way back when. He tried to hang on to that life, to avoid becoming an adult, but couldn't. Why did he lie during the chat? Was he ashamed that Valumart finally beat him? Or because he no longer saw much difference between the Dork and Light sides? A pocketful of loyal jelly had nothing to do with it; Valumart didn't kill him because he realized that Barry was *no longer his enemy*.

Without knowing it, sometime on that last quest with Lon and Ermine, Barry crossed the magical barrier from kid to adult. He started caring less about what he did, than what he got paid for doing it. Valumart let him go, Hogwash shut down, and Barry went into business with Uncle Serious.

Serious, Barry, J.G., Bumblemore – they all wanted money; that's all most of them thought about. Bumblemore was constantly hawking his 'How-To' magic-trick videos on late-night TV, Serious had a million schemes; J.G. had ground out book after book and Barry guilted her into giving him a piece of that. They all had a little Valumart in them, Barry included: that

arrogant, self-righteous, energetic, idealistic kid he was
at 22 was dead.

Or was he? Barry thought about what the actor
playing Valumart had said, how the movie would geld
the books. After all this, J.G.'s books seemed like the
only good, pure thing that remained. They gave joy.
They let their readers escape, and made their imagina-
tions stronger. And now the movie might change that.

He thought about the live-action version of *The Git
Who Stole Christmas*. How many kids had watched that
bloated pap, and never seen the elegant little cartoon it
was based on? Millions, probably. His life, and J.G.'s
books, might be blotted out by more cynical Hollywood garbage. Unless he did something about it. But
what? He pulled the videotape from his carry-on. He
couldn't stop the first movie, but he might be able to
stop *this* one.

The Concorde touched down; Barry had made his
decision. He wouldn't tell Ermine; any scheme would
be outrageously illegal, and she was always such a wet-
blanket about that. Behind the homecoming smiles, he
brooded, and by the time he arrived at the office the
next morning, he had developed the outlines of a plan.

'Phyllis,' Barry asked, 'could you get Severe Snipe
on the phone for me?'

'Certainly,' Phyllis said. She was the ex-President of

Barry's American fan club, and indispensable to him. Ermine teased him about his college-girl secretary, but she needn't have worried; if people were vegetables, Phyllis was celery – pleasant enough, but very little flavour. Moments later, she piped, 'Mr. Snipe is on line two, Mr. Trotter.'

Barry picked up the phone. 'Hello, Severe. I need to ask you a question.' 'Ask away.' Snipe, Barry's old professor, was now working for the Army on bio-magical warfare. Snipe had gotten a bad rap in the books, which made him into a villain more out of J.G.'s artistic necessity than any reality. He was all right, if you didn't mind a dusting of magic airborne gonorrhea now and then.

'Let's say I needed to make something absolutely unique,' Barry said. 'One-of-a-kind. Is there a spell for that?'

'Sure, there is. And it's not very hard, so you won't have to get Ermine to cast it for you!'

'Ha, yeah,' Barry said. On second thought, Snipe was a mild a-hole. 'Where can I find it?'

'Should be in Eccles' Standard Spellbook. If it's not, try Bluebottle's Potions, Hexes, and Charms. If you can't find it, call me back.' Snipe paused, then asked, 'How was America?'

'Somebody offered to buy my driver's license for $5,000.'

Snipe laughed. 'Well, I hope you took it.'

Barry thanked his old teacher for the information, and hung up. He looked at his watch – he would just make that Diviners meeting. As he walked through the front office, speech and slides tucked in his briefcase, he asked Phyllis to find him the appropriate spell. 'Will do,' she said. Phyllis was frighteningly efficient.

Looking out on a sea of Diviners' fezzes, he delivered his talk listlessly, mentally filling in the details of his plan. A Diviner gave him a ride back to the office in one of their tiny cars. Phyllis was still buried under a pile of books, some of them clearly quite ancient and magical (they fluoresced).

'Find anything?' Barry asked, hanging his coat up.

'Almost,' she said, twirling her hair with a finger as she always did when working. 'Alpo Bumblemore called, about the banquet.'

Barry thought about calling the weathered old berk, then put it off. He might wheedle the plan out of Barry, and feed him some line about breaking the law. He'd been ignoring that speech since age 11. 'I'll call him later,' he said.

'Aha!' Phyllis exclaimed. 'Is this what you want?' She handed him an open book. Garishly illuminated, it was made of vellum, and hummed faintly. 'Uncumber's Unique Unction,' Barry read. A quick skim convinced him that the spell would be perfect. He took the book into his office, and called back to Phyllis. 'Find me that videotape I brought back.'

She brought it in. 'You're not taking this home tonight, are you? I was going to have the Coven over to watch it.' The Coven was Phyllis' name for a bunch of American expat Trotter fanatics that lived in her neighbourhood. Occasionally one would pick her up from work, and Barry would be forced to pose for a picture or twelve. He didn't mind, Phyllis' friends were uniformly babes.

He took the tape. 'Don't worry, you guys will be able to watch it.'

'Mr. Trotter, what are you up to?'

'I'm going to make this copy unique. I won't be the crown jewel in somebody's marketing scheme,' Barry said. 'It's awful to have every aspect of your life fictionalised and turned into entertainment. I'm sick of it. It stops now.'

'Oh, Mr. Trotter!' Phyllis cried, 'You can't destroy the movie. So many people are looking forward to it.'

'Yeah, I talked to them yesterday, on the Internet. They're goofballs. Anyway, I'm not destroying it,' Barry said. 'There will still be one copy. You can do whatever you want with it once I'm finished. Watch it, circulate it, sell it – I don't care.'

'But why?' Phyllis asked, truly upset. 'You know how much people love your adventures!'

'Let them read the books, then,' Barry said. 'There's plenty of good stuff in those.' Remembering as much as he could from the speech he heard on the set, Barry said, 'Once this movie comes out, *it* will be Barry Trotter, not the books. We know the books are wonderful – what's the chance that this movie will come up to that standard? That kind of lightning doesn't strike twice.'

'But if the books are wonderful, isn't the more, the better?'

'Not necessarily. When you're reading the books, you provide the pictures. So not only do you tell yourself the story in a way that is meaningful – Bumblemore looks like your favorite Uncle – you also exercise your imagination while doing it.'

'Right, but—'

'So say I'm a kid who sees the movie, then picks up the books. Who's making the pictures then? The movie people! And since movies are a business – and a pretty cynical one at that – the pictures that they give you will be the blandest, most mainstream ones they can come up with. They'll put some market-researched, audi-ence-tested, focus-grouped crap into your head – and call it Barry Trotter!' Barry paused, shaking the videotape for emphasis. 'I'm Barry Trotter, and I say: *enough*! I'm not destroying the movie. I'm saving the books.'

Phyllis was quiet. Then she said, 'Mr. Trotter, not only do I think you'll have the world's biggest lawsuit on your hands' – Barry shrugged – 'but it won't change a thing.

'TV and movies is what people like today. Making it impossible for people to see this one movie won't change that. They'll just watch some other movie instead, and then there's *no* chance that they'll read the books. A lot more kids will pick up a copy if you let the movie happen. Look at *Citronella* – how many horrible things have been based on that poor fairy tale? But kids still read it.

'The best books have a life of their own, Mr. Trotter. And as much as we want to protect them from people who only want to make a quick buck, we can't force people to love them. Trust all the readers out there. They've done right by you so far.'

Now it was Barry's turn to sit quietly. Finally, he stood up and handed the tape to Phyllis. 'Take this away from me before I change my mind.' She smiled and took the tape. Another week, another harebrained scheme defused, Phyllis thought. Was this constant trickle of bad judgment a wizard thing? Anyway, she considered it part of the job. 'Thank you for trusting me, Mr. Trotter,' she said and left the room.

'It wasn't because I was afraid of getting sued!' he yelled after her.

Had he done the right thing? Barry had no idea. Suddenly, he felt very tired for someone who was only 27. He was right, all those years ago – adulthood was a drag. Then again, consider the alternative.

He called Alpo Bumblemore.

EPILOGUE

༄ཨ

Several weeks later, after the movie's triumphant – that is, mind-numbingly lucrative – appearance, Barry and Ermine buoyantly boarded the old Hogwash Express, en route to a fete the likes of which the school had never seen. Famous alumni, trustees, and other grand high muckety-mucks were converging on Hogwash from all directions, celebrating the dedication of the newly reopened school. The BBC was even making a documentary, 'The Remaking of Hogwash.'

The school's Trustees, always a greedy bunch, had loaned the old castle to Wagner Brothers for use in the movie. The script predictably called for the rotting old hulk to be blown up – and it was, extravagantly, in a scene the Trustees assumed was mostly special effects. To their horror, the studio returned not so much a school as a patch of blasted heath. The flabbergasted Trustees sued, and won a billion-dollar settlement.

Epilogue

After selling the rubble to Trotter fans hungry for 'a piece of Hogwash history,' the Trustees had enough cash to build a bigger, better, thoroughly modern and utterly charmless school on the same spot. 'Some might miss the quaint idiosyncracies of the old Hogwash, but the new facility is sure to charm with its plentiful amenities (hot water 24/7) and daring modern architecture,' the Hogwash Alumni Magazine chirped. 'It has Internet connections and an Olympic-sized swimming pool *not* infested by Groovylows.'

Barry hated it at first sight – all mirrored glass and chrome tubing in the shape of an immense wizard's hat. But others were working hard to make it friendlier. Even J.G. Rollins had gotten into the act, donating a new Quiddit field, already christened 'The Cauldron.'

As the Scottish scenery skimmed by, Barry kept reading. The lead story was about a statue donated to the school by Ludicrous Malfeasance in memory of his son, Dorco. Dorco, a classmate of Barry's, died after a tragic stupidity accident midway through his seventh year. The cover showed Ludicrous shaking hands with Lon Measly.

Lon had recently replaced old Bumblemore as Headmaster of the school. Simultaneously with the first movie imbroglio, the civil war between the mice and the bats had spiraled out of control, and poor Alpo had lost control of the school. Everyone had been driven out, and classes had to be suspended indefinitely, as both the mice and bats made themselves impossible to dislodge. Before the Wagner deal, the Trustees were seriously considering asking the Army to clear out what had become a rodential Masada.

But it had all worked out. Hogwash had never been more prosperous than under its new gladhanding idiot savant. Lon had a Laborador's loyalty and a Doberman's tenacity. He literally didn't know when to quit. Furthermore, Lon's affable vacancy had made him an ace fundraiser. If things continued like this, who knows where Lon Measly might end up, Barry thought. President of the United States?

It felt almost like school days again, as he and Ermine, Lon and his brothers all sat in the Grand Hall, eating and joking. The major topic of conversation was, as usual, Lord Valumart.

'I don't care how big a Dork Wizard you are, you can't outsmart Inland Revenue,' Bumblemore said. 'Trust me, I *know*!' After the school had closed down, Bumblemore had made the rounds of various conventions, signing memorabilia. He didn't declare a penny of that money, and Prissy Measly, the Eternal Prefect, had spilled the beans. Bumblemore's fame and years of service to society had kept him out of Aztalan, and he worked off his sentence doing magic for seniors at area nursing homes. Lon had made him Headmaster Emeritus. He was happy to practice his card tricks in peace and leave the education and discipline to others. Even Bumblemore's gnarled libido seemed under control.

Barry found the new Hogwash antiseptic, a feeling only encouraged by the garish and abrasive ads plastered all over the walls of the Grand Hall.

The Trustees had sold the space, and not cheaply, to various companies anxious to cultivate 'the next generation of wizards.' But a sterile Hogwash was better than none at all, and maybe the architecture grows on you, he thought.

As all around him chatted and clowned for the BBC's cameras, Bumblemore conjured at his turbot listlessly. After it had been cleared away, he turned to Barry and said, 'Trotter, may I have a word with you, in private?'

'Certainly.' Barry's natural response, learned after years of being yelled at, was to run.

They moved to a quiet alcove. 'Barry, we've been talking – that is, some of the Trustees have been thinking – er, Lonald has asked me to—'

'Spit it out,' Barry said, in a friendly tone, though

Bumblemore didn't seem to take it that way. He lost his temper, and the saliva began to fly.

'Blackstone's britches! I can't do it – not after all the crap you and your cronies have pulled over the years! You sold the map in the first place, then didn't stop the movie—'

'Did you have something to say, or did you invite me over here simply for purposes of abuse?' Barry asked, with a smile. The old man, after all, had every right, and Barry was too giddy from the strong and plentiful wine (from Hafwid's new vinyard, co-owned with Francis Bored Coppola) to give a tinker's dam.

Bumblemore collected himself, took a deep breath, and said it all in a rush, like someone ripping off a very painful plaster. 'The Trustees have asked me to ask you to consider joining us as Hogwash's new Public Relations Officer.'

Barry was surprised. Bumblemore continued, unhappily making his case. 'We'd pay you something, though clearly not as much as you could make in the private sector. We – they – just feel that building the image of the new place is important, and you're the one alumnus best suited to exploit the media,' Bumblemore said. 'It pains me to say this, but I think there's a place for you at the new Hogwash.'

Barry didn't need time to think. 'Yes, of course!' he

said, grabbing the old wizard's hand, which had been hanging unenthusiastically at his side. 'It's a deal.'

'Good, good,' Bumblemore said, his voice filled with dread at the trouble a wealthy, adult Barry Trotter could cause. 'Now if you'll excuse me, I think that turbot was tinged with Dork magic . . .'

Barry returned to his seat at the banquet, which was racheting itself steadily higher. Mrs. McGoogle had turned into a cat and was leaping from table to table merrily. Ferd and Jorge were telling the story of their revenge on Zed Grimfood; they had set up a scam which had resulted in him being caught with an underaged elf. Zed's misfortune was met with gales of laughter. Garrulous gluttony cascaded all around he and Ermine.

'Did he finally ask you?' Ermine asked.

'You knew?'

'Of course. You better have said yes – I told them I'd be the next head of Grittyfloor, starting at the beginning of term.' Ermine said.

Barry smiled. It was amazing how great things were turning out. He'd get to be at Hogwash forever. He hugged his bride-to-be tightly. 'This is going to be great,' Barry gushed. 'We're going to have so much fun.'

'I know what you call "fun," Trotter,' Ermine teased. 'I'm running a House, not an asylum.'

The following autumn was one of the best anyone could remember. The students loved their new school, the few who missed the funky ambiance of the old Hogwash being more than won over by the lightning-fast connections to Internet porn and working showers. And of course there was Barry and Ermine's wedding out by the lake, with the sea monster acting as ringbearer, snaking its lo-o-ong tentacle into the proceedings at the appropriate moment, dropping the ring into Barry's palm. Of the Measly-orchestrated reception in Hogsbleede, suffice it to say that by night's end, the jails were filled with the couple's friends and relations.

After a luxurious honeymoon at J.G. Rollins' pseudo-Carribbean estate, the couple eventually resumed their duties at Hogwash. Ermine had, to nobody's surprise, taken to her new job immediately, ordering everyone about with relish. Barry had a tougher problem to solve: he'd made his peace with there being several decades' worth of Trotter films, but they took so damn long to make. How, then, could he keep the school in the public eye, until the next one was squeezed from Hollywood's withered loins? The Okrah show was only worth so many visits . . .

The answer came to him one crisp morning in October, as he watched the Grittyfloor Quiddit squad practice a few illegal manuevers: he would write a *parody*, based around the adventures of himself and his friends! It would be clumsy sometimes, but heck, the bar was pretty low for that kind of thing.

As he walked back from The Cauldron, kicking up piles of bright orange leaves, the ideas came fast and furious. At his brand-new desk, Barry set his phone to voice mail, turned on his computer, and began to write: 'The Hogwash School for Wizards was the most famous school in the wizarding world, and Barry Trotter was its most famous student . . .'

The end.[17]

---

[17] I've been reading this over, and I have to say that I have no idea what's going on. First, it's a book about a movie. Then, the book turns out to have been a movie all along – about trying to stop an earlier movie. Now it's all a parody written by Barry Trotter HIMSELF? Kids, let this be a warning to you: postmodern tools in the wrong hands (*i.e.*, mine) can be *deadly*. If you know – or even *think* you know – what I might be getting at with all this, please print your explanation legibly in ink on a 3x5 card, and eat it. Ha, ha, just kidding: send it to me, care of the publisher. We can still save this book! Send your solution today!

SPECIAL SECRET
BONUS!

⟨∞⟩

I realize that many of you may have been offended or confused by this book. Younger readers might even have been turned-off reading for *good*. That's a real shame, but the hectic pace of modern life makes taking time out to tell me a thing or two impossible. So, as a heartfelt thank you for making it all the way to the end, I have written a generic letter of offense that can be photocopied and mailed to me at your leisure. Enjoy, and thanks again for reading *Barry Trotter and the Shameless Parody!*

I HATE YOU!

Dear Sir:

I was very offended by your book *Barry Trotter and the Shameless Parody*. I am …

(tick all that apply)

❏ an overprotective Potter fan
❏ an outraged parent
❏ a confused preteen
❏ a world-weary 15-year old
❏ an unamused copyright holder
❏ J.K. Rowling
❏ an embittered fellow humourist
❏ an aspiring assassin
❏ an ex-girlfriend

I am writing to say how appalled I was at your …

❏ turning something wonderful into something sordid
❏ unrelenting scatology
❏ shaky grasp of grammar, spelling and syntax (note no serial comma)
❏ inept plotting
❏ reliance on cheap meta-tricks
❏ irritating characters that sound all the same
❏ cheap-ass paper
❏ getting drunk and calling me, asking to get back together
❏ teaching my young child about 'water sports' for God's sake

contd overleaf

How does it feel, Mr Gerber, to be …

- ❏ a shameless parasite?
- ❏ crippled by an oppressive cynicism?
- ❏ the defendent
- ❏ a poisoner of fresh, young minds?
- ❏ clearly history's greatest monster?
- ❏ immature beyond belief?
- ❏ Mr King Ripper-Offer?
- ❏ on Jesus Christ's 'official shit list'?
- ❏ the only one whose sacrifices will STOP the VOICES

I hope you're happy now, jerk-o.
Cordially yours,